HAUNTED
BISBEE

HAUNTED BISBEE

FRANCINE POWERS

FOREWORD BY DEBE BRANNING

HAUNTED
America

Published by Haunted America
A Division of The History Press
Charleston, SC
www.historypress.com

First published 2020

Manufactured in the United States

ISBN 9781467145619

Library of Congress Control Number: 2020938482

My three children, Brittany, Chelsie and Grant, and my grandchildren, Andre and Olive—you have all inspired me to write about our hometown and its history with love and reverence. My husband, Randy—I thank you for gifting me the time to take on this project and encouraging me to do so.

To the generations of my family who have worked in the Bisbee copper mines: my grandfather Alfred Quen; my dad, Matias V. Rojas; and two of my mother's brothers.

To all who have had the privilege of living in Bisbee and are interested in its past, I wholeheartedly dedicate these writings to you and all other generations that pass through or are lucky enough to live there.

CONTENTS

CONTENTS

FOREWORD

What better way to explore the ghosts of Bisbee than through the eyes of a true native of this historic and all-so-spooky town! Francine grew up learning the legends of the mighty mining town from her mother and family, who were also born and raised there. The ghosts of Bisbee know Francine as well as she knows them.

As a reporter for the local newspapers, she learned that credibility is the key attribute of a reputable journalist. Researching every story for truth and accuracy is a must for a great read. I first met Francine sometime in February 2000, when my paranormal team, MVD Ghostchasers, came down to research stories for my first book, *Sleeping with Ghosts*. The Bisbee newspaper sent Francine along to write a story about the adventure. While the ghost hunters documented their paranormal experiences with tools of the trade, little did I know that Francine was seeing and observing these encounters in real time. I did not know early on that she could "see" the spirits! A gifted medium, Francine has communicated with the dead most of her life, the ghosts of Bisbee being near and dear to her.

We did not see each other for a few years but kept in touch via email and the internet. She published her book *Mi Reina: Don't Be Afraid*; my book had finally been published close to the same time. We arranged to meet again down in Bisbee. Remarkably, we learned that we had experienced a similar encounter (in completely different decades) with the spirit of a young boy in the city park—site of the first cemetery in Bisbee.

I have dabbled on an unfinished manuscript about a young girl growing up in the early 1900s in Bisbee, during its most prosperous days. If I had a question on a time or location for the book, it was like Francine was one step ahead of me with an answer. Had we known each other in a previous lifetime and were simply recalling some of our early years?

When I was asked to be a part of an internet series, Streets of Fear, covering Tombstone Canyon Road, which flows through the city, I immediately contacted Francine. Together, we covered the Inn at Castle Rock, Fire Station No. 2 and the scary tale of her being chased by some unseen entity down Tombstone Canyon Road on the way to elementary school. Francine was also asked to talk about Bisbee spirits on TV's *Ghost Hunters* and I have appeared on *Ghost Adventures*. Thankfully, we have been the go-to people in our localities and have enjoyed it over the years.

After purchasing my weekend home in Bisbee in April 2007, Francine became a member of MVD Ghostchasers to help cover the Bisbee area. We were able to investigate some of the old, historical buildings and explore the deserted Camp Naco nearby. Francine also started her own online magazine, *Spirits of Cochise Country*, for which I was a part-time contributing author. Again, every detail in her work was researched and accurate in both Cochise County and Bisbee history.

Recently, she owned and hosted Bisbee Historical Tours and Bisbee Historical Haunted Cart Tours for several years, offering real ghost stories, and she was featured on many local newscasts promoting the informative tours. The haunted tour operated in golf carts and escorted guests to locations with original spooky tales.

It is important to remember that *anyone* can tell a ghost story—but it takes someone special like Francine Powers to *live* a ghost story and bring it to life. Sit tight! *Haunted Bisbee* is that sort of book! It will soon become your second eyes to the ghosts of "old Bisbee."

—Debe Branning
MVD Ghostchasers
Paranormal investigator/author

PREFACE

I am a married mother of three, a grandmother and an Arizona Foundation Newspaper award-winning reporter. I'm also a Mexican American and a several-generation Bisbee native. Writing *Haunted Bisbee* has been a long time coming, as this is not my first book about ghosts in Bisbee. *Mi Reina: Don't Be Afraid*, published in 2004, is an original journal about growing up with the paranormal in the small town. It is also the first book of its kind covering haunted sites in Bisbee.

I penned explicit details about the paranormal activity that surrounded me at six years of age in my childhood home and how the Tucson Diocese of the Roman Catholic Church became involved. I wrote of how I used to hide under my blankets in terror when ghosts surrounded my bedside and how I testified to becoming a medium from early adolescence.

I wrote about my older twin sisters playing with the Ouija board—a spirit board game—and the ensuing explosion of terrifying paranormal activity that was unleashed, setting a precedent for the rest of the book.

In recent years, I owned Bisbee Historical Tours and gave walking tours in the day and in the evening. I also operated Bisbee Historical Haunted Cart Tours. I leased gas-powered golf carts from another tour company in town. We put LED lights in the roofs and ran the carts over the steep, hilly roads at night. I based that tour on my book and on additional intensely researched sites, such as Bisbee Fire Station No. 2. I was allowed to conduct the first ghost hunt there and broke that ghost story in 2009. My husband, Randy, and I ran the tour business for a few years, then relocated to Tucson, Arizona.

I wrote editorials for the *Bisbee Observer* regarding haunted Bisbee sites. I wrote about Bisbee Fire Station No. 2 in the paper in 2013; in 2015, I wrote about the Bisbee Oliver House. I included substantial information about the mysterious death of Nat Anderson and other resident ghosts there.

I also owned an online magazine, *Spirits of Cochise County*, in 2009. It covered haunted sites throughout the county and included old ghost stories and other stories I originated, which are still being used today.

When the television show *Ghost Hunters* came to Bisbee, it had me on in 2006. For about two decades, I've been on several radio and television shows as well as podcasts to talk about Bisbee's history and haunted sites.

Bisbee has many ghost stories, but only the true haunted stories carry any weight in the paranormal world. I'm a big naysayer to fake stories and those people who showboat and cover ill-researched ghost stories to make a quick buck. It's not fair when paranormal investigators are given untrue information. No one wants to chase fake ghosts.

It's vital to stick to real history to keep Bisbee's historical district intact. A way to ensure that is the way I have written *Haunted Bisbee*. This book covers the town's earliest haunted history to the present day, with the prudence and veneration that people who have walked its streets for about 140 years deserve.

INTRODUCTION

Bisbee, a small town in the southwestern part of the United States, is a place that, if you drove on its curvy twists and turns of roads, you might feel as if you were floating back in time. Above the streets, etched into the middle of a canyon, are houses clinging to the mountainsides and hilly neighborhoods. They feature layers upon layers of different colors in a turn-of-the-twentieth-century style. It's a mining community that was once proudly hailed as the "Queen of Copper Camps." The company town was sculpted by the movement of mountain and rock, backbreaking labor and implausible determination. Bisbee, Arizona, has been continuously filled with generations of valiant people who lived through outbreaks of typhoid fever and meningitis. They survived fires, floods and the fall of its great mining industry in 1975 and now have reinvented the town as an artist community.

Before the city of Bisbee was founded, the area had a thick growth of timber, was lush with manzanita bushes and had an array of wildlife. The area was called the Southern Dragoon Mountains and, at the time, was considered to be Apache territory. There was a trail through the mountains that had a desert spring, which was also the only water source for the Apaches traveling from the Sulphur Springs Valley. This spring was documented as early as 1848.

Almost thirty years later, in 1877, deep into these mountains, saw the arrival of U.S. Army lieutenant John A. Rucker with fifteen men of Company C, Sixth Cavalry, from Fort Bowie, along with John "Jack" Dunn. They were on an expedition to see if members of the Chiricahua Apache tribe had an encampment in the area. Dunn was considered to be the best scout at the fort under General George Cook.

Lieutenant Rucker and his group camped overnight at the first spring they came upon. After their night there, Dunn walked farther up the canyon in search of better drinking water; the soldiers had complained of the other spring's quality and taste. He spotted a fresh spring flowing over a huge mountainous rock, now christened "Castle Rock." It was the same water source the Apaches had used for decades.

He filled his containers with fresh water and headed back to camp. As he traveled down the north side of the barely visible trail, he spotted a green-tinted stain on the east side of an enormous rock. This may have been an indication of the presence of lead, copper and silver. He took some samples and went directly back to notify Rucker of his discovery.

After hearing the promising news, the entire party broke camp and went straight to the spring at the base of Castle Rock. Shortly after, Rucker, Dunn and their packer, T.D. Byrne, claimed the first mine in this area on August 2, 1877. They called it the Rucker. They registered the claim in Tucson, as the area at the time was considered to be in Pima County.

Early Castle Rock, near where Jack Dunn discovered evidence of what was to be one of the grandest copper mines in history.

A few weeks later, a prospector with a long life of trauma and drama named George Warren was grubstaked by Dunn to find more rich spots in the area. This was because Dunn was contracted to the military and didn't have the freedom to schedule his time to prospect some more. In return, Warren was to name Dunn in all notices of places he might find. Warren found more claims but never listed Dunn on any of the several he located.

The abrasive prospector was born in Massachusetts around 1835. After his mother died, he joined his father in New Mexico, where an Indian war party killed his father and where he was kidnapped by the group. He was a young boy at the time and was held for eighteen months by his captors. He was traded for fifteen pounds of sugar to two traveling prospectors who recognized him as white. He learned a great deal of prospecting from his two saviors and later, through odd jobs, gained mining experience.

Only fifty-six days after the Rucker Mine had been discovered, Warren found a second mining claim in the area, naming it the Mercy Mine. He is considered by some to be the "Father of Bisbee."

Years later, Warren gambled several claims in a footrace against a horse in Charleston, Arizona. He lost that race and, eventually, the rest of his claims, worth millions of dollars, to deceitful and greedy business partners. In the last years of his life, he worked at different saloons, sweeping floors and cleaning spittoons.

In 1917, a grand monument to Warren was placed in Evergreen Cemetery with a plaque reading, "Poor in Purse Rich in Friends."

The famous photographer C.S. Fly eternalized Warren when a photograph he took of the infamous prospector was used for the model of a miner for the Arizona State Seal in 1912.

Soon after Warren made his discoveries, several mining corporations came rushing to the area, which was finally named the Mule Mountains. The most dominant companies in the long run were the Copper Queen Company, Phelps Dodge and Company (PD) and the Calumet and Arizona Mining Company (C&A Mining Company). In 1885, PD merged with the Copper Queen Company as the Copper Queen Consolidated Company. Calumet developed one of the most outrageously rich mines, called the Irish Mag. In 1931, the C&A Mining Company merged with Phelps Dodge.

The booming mining camp was named in honor of Judge DeWitt Bisbee of the mining firm Williams and Bisbee of San Francisco. He loaned $20,000 to the engineering firm Martin and Ballard to buy the Copper Queen prospect. This was to be the largest and most productive mine in the area. If you can believe it, the judge never took a step in the town named for him.

1917 George Warren monument in Evergreen Cemetery, built with a collection of monies from the local Elks Club.

Bisbee quickly went from a mining camp with tents sprawled across its canyons to an established town with restaurants, saloons, boardinghouses and rental shacks. It even had its share of brothels, gambling establishments and opium dens. These institutions were mostly saturated in an area of town called Brewery Gulch.

It was important to families of the miners to have a school for the children in the camp and for them to be educated in the new part of the Arizona Territory and newly created Cochise County. A committee was created in 1881 to create a school district. Bisbee became County School District No. 2, while Tombstone was named No. 1.

Clara J. Stillman, Bisbee's first schoolteacher. She was a hardy soul and a brave woman who managed to get through school lessons regardless of distressing "Indian drills."

The first postmaster of Bisbee, Horace C. Stillman, was also chairman of the newly formed school trustees committee. Coincidentally, he had a sister who had just graduated from a Connecticut teachers' academy and would be perfect as the first educator in the mining town.

Clara J. Stillman, Bisbee's first schoolteacher, arrived in 1881. She was offered a tiny unused miner's shack to teach a class of five near Castle Rock. The first day of school was October 3, five days after her arrival. The school was there for only about four weeks before mayhem took place. A group of Apache men had driven off several pastured horses positioned near and above the schoolhouse.

Due to the fear and concern for the safety for the teacher and students, the school was moved to the Miners Union Hall at the entrance of Brewery Gulch. Just in that little time, Stillman's class grew to twelve students.

Safety measures were taken to the extreme, and an Indian drill was created as a cautionary measure against attacks from local bands of Native Americans. A code was established: four blasts—two short and one long and then one short again—from the work whistle at the Copper Queen Mine. The pupils were directed to hold hands and follow Miss Stillman to the designated shelter, which was always supplied with food and water. The Copper Queen Mine, or what was later to be called the Glory Hole tunnel, was the spot. These drills ended when the famed Chiricahua Apache named Geronimo was captured in 1886.

The Bisbee District was booming. Men from all parts of the country and world came looking for a job or a claim strike. They came from Germany, Mexico, Poland, England, Italy, Serbia and Ireland. The average pay for a Bisbee miner at its early stages was about $3.50 a day. By 1920, it was $6.00 per hour. The average pay today for a copper miner can average from $65,000 to $73,000 per year.

With the increase in population and mining success came some dissatisfactory situations, such as the thick smoke of pollution coming from the flumes of the copper smelter, located almost in the heart of the city.

Because of the many restaurants, saloons, markets, hotels and houses placed in every nook and cranny of the narrow canyons, there were tons of garbage and raw sewage in some of the streets. The stench of the open sewage pits and the trash that was thrown out was horrendous. Owners of restaurants even threw carcasses of butchered animals into the alleys, where they decomposed, adding to the poor living conditions. All of these situations caused millions of flies to populate the area, triggering a great deal of health issues. Bisbee also had to contend with extreme flash floods from the monsoon rains and several devastating fires.

Regardless of these problems, the mines were producing about one million pounds of ore a month and had to transport one hundred tons a day by an eighteen-mule team to the town of Fairbanks, which had the nearest train station, then on to Benson. Production was so good that the mining companies could afford to transport the ore to a smelter in Phoenixville, Pennsylvania.

At first, the mule teams would go around the San Pedro Valley to get to Fairbanks. P.H. Banning's place was a watering stop for the mules and drivers. Banning suggested that a road be built over the Mule Mountains. He was awarded the contract to build the road, which took about nine months to finish.

Incredibly, a mule skinner would drive the team up and over the treacherous mountain with precise skill and with very little room for another horse or wagon to pass. Eventually, this way of transporting ore became embarrassing for the mining company. A Fowler tractor engine was used to substitute the mules; sadly, it would often tip over and get stuck.

The New Mexico & Arizona Railroad built a railway from the new main Southern Pacific line from the town of Benson, then south to Fairbank, which was along the San Pedro River. Finally, in 1889, Phelps Dodge built the Arizona & Southeastern Railroad from Fairbank, all the way to Bisbee. In 1901, the El Paso & Southwestern Railroad Company bought the railway. This valuable extension to Bisbee was a huge factor in the increase in production of copper and other minerals.

After the railroad extension, there was an increase in population and a large economy to support it. Railroad lines were extending and connecting for both freight and passenger services. Luckily for Bisbee residents, the passenger services reached the new urban community.

In November 1903, an old freight train depot was dismantled to make room for a new passenger-freight combination depot. The five-stall roundhouse of crenelated sheet iron was located at the foot of OK Street. The overall length of the new depot was two hundred feet. The waiting room and ticket office were at the west end of the structure. On the site of

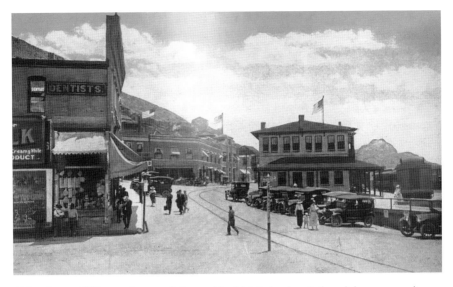

Bisbee Depot, lifeline to the rest of the world, which helped push the mining community into modern times.

the former roundhouse were the baggage and express offices. The part of the building that handled freight was on the spot where the turntable and lead tracks were formerly located.

There were thirty windows on the second floor, where the offices would have lots of sunlight. The two-story depot was completed on May 17, 1905. The passenger terminal opened to the public on June 24 and stayed open until 1951.

Sheila Goar, daughter of William "Bill" Goar and Grace Brownlie Goar, said during an interview with me that she had grand memories of growing up in Bisbee and recalled the time when the train was running. Sheila, who was born in 1940, said, "When the train came in, we all knew it. A 'click, click, click' sound would be heard down from the mountain where the pit is now. The whistle would blow and when the train hooked up cars it made a big banging noise. We always knew when people were getting shipments. Either Phelps Dodge or another business were getting a load or something of interest."

The railroad into Bisbee made it possible for fresh seafood and oysters and other finer things—exquisite furniture, material for clothing and every dry-goods item imaginable—from California and the East Coast to be delivered to Bisbee during the Edwardian era. Bisbee was quickly becoming a town of high society and houses and buildings filled with luxury.

While Bisbee was quickly resembling a Gilded Age town, the smelter for the Bisbee mines was very noisy and polluted, not to mention the foul air being pushed wherever the wind took it. In 1902, to finally solve this unpleasant situation, the minds of the mining corporation created a small city named Douglas about twenty-five miles southeast of Bisbee to house a modernized smelter operation.

Different mines were continuously being discovered, and the town began to stretch out into suburbs and satellite communities. An area known as Lowell was formed in 1901. Other neighborhoods such as Jiggerville, located on Sacramento Hill, were created. Shift bosses were called "jigger bosses," and this is the community where they lived. Upper Lowell was created soon after. South Bisbee was another suburb, and the Warren District was soon developed.

The C&A Mining Company decided that the nationally acclaimed City Beautiful movement would be an excellent model for the new townsite of Warren. The new area, named after "good ole" George Warren, is about three miles southeast of Bisbee. It was completed around 1907. Other notable areas that sprang up in later Bisbee history include San Jose, Bakerville, Briggs, Don Luis, Galena, Tintown and Saginaw.

Bisbee was always at the cusp of modernization. A good example of this was the construction of the Warren-Bisbee Railway beginning in the year 1907 by the C&A Mining Company. The electric trolley system was in demand because of the great walking distance between Bisbee, Lowell and Warren. In the same year, the link from Warren to Lowell was completed, and in March 1908, the railway reached Bisbee. The hop-on, hop-off transit's fare was five cents, and ladies rode for free on opening day. The streetcars ran from 5:00 a.m. to 2:00 a.m., with the schedule attempting to keep in sync with the mining shifts to accommodate miners.

The Warren Company, a subsidiary of the C&A Mining Company, ran the railway. There were twelve streetcars, including six McGuire-Cummings interurban cars. An extension to the line in 1909 made its way up Tombstone Canyon as far as a popular market called Moore's Grocery. In 1910, the railway's final destination was constructed, even farther up the road, with an upper termination point at Tombstone Canyon and Pace Avenue. The original trolley stop, which is a bench made of stone, still exists.

Sadly, this dashing and exciting way of travel ended for Bisbee residents in May 1928. At this time, the track, streetcars and overhead electric lines were all in need of repair. A public vote of 448 to 35 decided to move the town into the modern era of buses. The new form of transportation, the

Left: Motorman's hat ornament from the Warren-Bisbee Railway. This archaic piece of Bisbee's interesting past was found in the desert area of High Lonesome Road.

Below: An original Warren-Bisbee Railway trolley stop, which eventually switched to a Warren-Bisbee Bus Line stop in 1928.

Warren-Bisbee Bus Line, replaced the trolleys with four Studebaker buses, each capable of holding twenty-one passengers.

A major event for Bisbee miners and residents took place on July 12, 1917: the Bisbee Deportation. The Industrial Workers of the World (IWW), or Wobblies, presented a list of demands to the Phelps Dodge and Calumet & Arizona mining companies. The mining officials refused those requests. As a result, the Bisbee Miners Union called a strike on June 24, and by June 27, half of the Bisbee workforce was on strike.

The Wobblies were connected to aggressive and intimidating crimes in Bisbee committed over the course of about three weeks. Due to these actions, Cochise County sheriff Harry C. Wheeler wrote an open letter and put it in the *Bisbee Daily Review* on July 12, 1917. In the letter, he warned all women and children to keep off the streets that day. He said that he formed a posse of twelve hundred men in Bisbee and one thousand in Douglas. He said he did this for the sole purpose of arresting strikers on charges of vagrancy, treason and of being disturbers of the peace.

The Wobblies' usual time for picketing was at 6:30 a.m., and a main gathering place was in front of the Bisbee United States Post Office. But on July 12, 1917, the streets and alleys of Bisbee were bursting with heavily armed citizens. As the Wobblies picketed, a whistle blew and an armed man emerged from the post office, another came out from the alley in the rear of the building and another jumped from the alley on Subway Street. The Wobblies, completely surrounded, surrendered without hesitation.

Deputized men scanned every possible hiding place a striker could be. When a large enough number was gathered in front of the post office, Sheriff Wheeler gave the order for the men to march.

The procession followed the train tracks to Lowell. As they walked, armed guards were on each side of the strikers. Miners just getting off shift ran home and grabbed their guns and joined the procession, which moved south toward the Warren Ball Park.

The strikers entered the park and poured through the open northwest gate. They filled up the grandstand, which overflowed to the baseball diamond. Armed guards surrounded the entire park. A freight engine with twenty-three boxcars and cattle cars with whistles blowing arrived at 11:00 a.m.

A last chance of choosing to work or to continue to strike was given. Those who chose to work were hustled out as the order to load the Wobblies was made. The men were lined up; approximately twelve hundred were loaded and ready to be hauled to Columbus, New Mexico. The train started up and headed toward a government-maintained camp, where they were to be dropped off.

Incredibly, the only incidents of the entire proceedings were the fatal shootings of O.P. McRae and James Brew. President Woodrow Wilson set up the Federal Mediation Commission to investigate. In the report, made by his special labor commission, it stated that the deportation was wholly illegal and without authority in law, either state or federal. It was found that no federal law applied here. It was referred to the State of Arizona, that such events be made criminal by federal statute. In the end, the mining company was placed at fault, boosting the efforts of the IWW.

Present mountain view of "Old Bisbee" and the Lavender Pit in the background.

New ways to mine ore were always being explored. In 1917, Bisbee's first open pit was created, and the ore was mined by steam shovels. The Sacramento Pit reached a depth too difficult to recover ore and closed its operations in September 1929. Mining administrators didn't give up on surface mining, so, in 1954, the Lavender Pit was created. It lasted much longer than the prior one and closed in December 1974. The pit was named after Harrison Lavender, a general manager of the Copper Queen Branch. Sadly, he died before it began production.

To make room for the open pits, houses had to be removed before blasting. These houses were relocated to surrounding neighborhoods, such as Galena and Saginaw. The structures were on stilts, not on foundations.

What follows are some interesting Bisbee facts. It was founded in 1880 and incorporated in 1902. The town's first elected mayor was Josiah Murihead, an immigrant from Canada. In 1929, the county seat was changed from Tombstone to Bisbee. There are 2,300 miles of mine tunnels under Bisbee, Lowell and Warren. During Bisbee's mining period, over three million ounces of gold and eight billion pounds of copper were extricated. Bisbee's elevation is 5,300 feet. The original segment of Bisbee and its residential area became a historical district in 1980. The mines and surrounding properties were solely owned in later years by Phelps Dodge and are now owned by Freeport McMoRan Copper and Gold.

Bisbee is now an eclectic town filled with charm and diverse cultures, surrounded by gorgeous Victorian structures and breathtaking mountainous views. The streets and hills are filled with an eerie presence of long ago. Bisbee is a living testament to a rich history and a colorful future.

1

TOMBSTONE CANYON ROAD

The history of early Bisbee includes not only the young and old pioneers of the mining camp but also lively characters who have left clear psychic flashes at several sites in and around town. Tombstone Canyon is a neighborhood where ghostly visitations have distressed residents for decades. The road is located at the higher altitude of Bisbee. It is the stretch of road that leads to Tombstone, Arizona, about twenty-two miles away—the reason it was named Tombstone Canyon Road. This was Bisbee's first urban neighborhood.

SPIRIT-LADEN HOUSE

At Upper Tombstone Canyon, you will find gorgeous, tall cottonwood trees and cool, fresh air blowing through the branches and leaves. During monsoon season, you might hear a light rush of running water in the deep ditches. Near the turnoff to Highway 80, and at the end of another narrow and extremely steep road, stands an original Bisbee house. This structure originally built around 1890 has been home to only a handful of families. Another house was built in 1928 on the same site. This is my childhood home.

Among the first people to live there was a couple. They were from different parts of the country and married in 1906 in Bisbee. She was from South Carolina; he had recently migrated to Colorado. The two corresponded for

Tombstone Canyon, an upscale neighborhood of early Bisbee. It is the neighborhood with the highest elevation and has annual snowfall and gorgeous mountainous views.

a year until they met in Arizona. The thirty-something woman traveled to Bisbee by train to meet her soon-to-be groom, who was a miner. The two had a lovely life and five children but stayed in the house for only a few years before relocating.

My parents bought that house in the late 1960s. It was the first place I lived in and the first place I experienced life with the supernatural.

At the time of the home's paranormal height of activity, I was entering the first grade. I had three older sisters and one brother at the time. My two eldest sisters are identical twins. The Ouija board was very popular in the early 1970s, and the twins decided to get their hands on it. Almost simultaneously, the paranormal occurrences began. When my mother found out, she took that game board and went outside and broke it on her knee. That didn't seem to stop the haunting.

Phantasm footsteps from different parts of the house were heard in the middle of the night, and the lights would flicker on and off at unexpected moments. One of my sisters said she was watching TV and, in the reflection of its screen, saw a figure walk behind her when no one else was in the room. She also saw puffs of cigarette smoke appearing out of thin air. My father said he heard a ball bouncing in my bedroom. He went to scold the person he thought was playing with it (me), but no one was there. Another sister claimed that she heard our mother washing dishes and yelled to her for water. When Mom didn't answer, she checked on her. No one was at the sink doing such a chore.

Eerie situations were happening at the house every day and night. I experienced the haunting but in a more personal way. I felt a warm and sweet connection with the spirit. At certain times, I could hear a younger woman sing. Her voice was pleasant. She was always near. But there was another entity in the home. He was an angry, jealous and violent male presence. I didn't like him and was terrified when I felt his company.

One night, I awoke to a slender figure at the side of my bed. I called out the names of my two teenaged twin sisters. The figure moved from the side of my bed and stood behind a lampshade on a nearby nightstand. The figure did not exert any negative vibrations.

"What?" I asked. The figure's long, tapered fingers clung to the lampshade as her head turned side to side. She seemed as confused as me.

I watched her move and could hear her hard shoes on the wood floor. She took a few steps back, and the floor creaked. She moved into the moonlight shining from our opened bedroom window. The curtains were billowing behind her. Suddenly, I could see all of her. Her hair was in a tight chignon held by a large comb. Her eyes were gentle. She had on a long-sleeved blouse with the collar up to her neck, hiding every inch of her skin. She had a tiny waist and wore a long skirt reaching down to her laced-up ankle boots. She was lovely.

I realized it wasn't one of my sisters and put my head on my pillow without breaking our gaze. Then she took two more steps back and put her hands in a praying position. She bowed her head, then penetrated the floor, gliding down and out of my sight!

The other ghost made appearances in much more dramatic ways. During a dinner, our five dogs started to bark and howl outside. Then suddenly, the sound of tin cans being dragged around the house erupted. We all stared at one another in shock. Then above our heads in the attic were the sounds of a physical fistfight. My father got up from the dinner table and went directly to the door that leads to the attic. He yelled up the steep set of stairs, "Who's there?" There was no answer, and the brawl stopped.

My parents decided to call the local priest the next day. Reverend Gilbert Padilla was the priest from our Roman Catholic church, St. Patrick's. He served at the church from 1970 to 1976. He came to do a house blessing. During that afternoon visit, he went to each room and threw holy water as he recited prayers of protection and for the release of any suppressed spirit residing there. He gave Holy Communion to my parents and blessed the children individually.

This made things calm for a little while, but not completely. My mother was taking an afternoon nap and woke up to an eyeless face floating on her bedroom wall. This caused my parents to call Father Padilla for another house blessing. He was not available, so the diocese sent a substitute. The next day, Reverend Thomas D. Rice, who would later serve at St. Patrick's Church from 1977 to 1981, arrived.

In no more than mere moments later, the sound of another fight started in the attic. The priest asked how to get up there. My father led him to the attic door. He opened it for him, and Father Rice made the sign of the cross and went up the stairs as my father followed. The priest began to pray. As he got to the third step from the top, he stopped, and his voice grew louder. He turned and extended his arm to my father to halt. The priest's blood seemed to drain from his face. When he reached the top, he looked like he was going to faint. He mustered his courage and took a few steps into the attic. The fighting stopped. The priest turned toward the stairs and hurried to exit. Suddenly, he was pushed and flew toward all of us at the bottom of the stairs! He fell into the wall and collapsed on the steps.

After that, Father Rice said he was going to recommend a special mass for further protection for our family and was going to meet with Father Padilla on his return. "I will discuss what has happened and the urgency of the situation. I am also going to recommend an exorcism," said the priest to my parents.

As an adult and in the late 1990s, I interviewed Reverend Stanley J. Nadolny, who was St. Patrick's pastor at that time. Father Nadolny said that since his arrival he had performed about twelve house blessings in Bisbee but denied ever witnessing an exorcism during his service there. The priest explained that the bishop from the diocese must give permission for an exorcism to take place. There are appointed exorcists to perform the solemn rituals called Major Exorcism and Simple Exorcism to drive out evil spirits in the name of the Church.

Father Nadolny explained that spirits do not possess homes or objects, because they have no souls. Exorcism is meant to drive out demons or dark spirits from the bodies and souls of the living and has a lingering outcome on houses and sites where paranormal sightings have occurred. The Bisbee priest said, "A Major Exorcism is for the express purpose of exorcizing diabolical spirits from the body of man." He added that the exorcist who entered our home may have read a Simple Exorcism prayer to free our family of the entities.

The bishop from the Tucson Diocese approved the religious event, and it did take place in the house on the hill and up Tombstone Canyon. It began with a mass in our living room. The officiant was positioned near the floor heater that had earlier been tagged as some sort of vortex. As the priest recited his sermon, I began to hear *her* sing again, ever so faintly.

The priest said: "I will recite the words of this prayer and walk through each room of the house as I bless each corner with holy water. Each of you will follow me close behind. Fear nothing, for Christ is here."

As the reverend walked, I noticed he had a crucifix placed in the seam of his book. As he began to whip holy water from his silver scepter, I also heard a quiet wind begin to blow. As he walked through the kitchen, a slamming door echoed throughout the house. He paused then continued to the next room.

The house seemed to tremble, and now I could hear wind howling in my ear. The priest stopped in different places along his route and read louder. The windows in my parents' bedroom began to vibrate, then shake. He ignored the dramatic scene and continued to walk through the house.

We reached the living room again and he stopped dead in his tracks as the laundry room door whipped open and slammed shut! The holy man grabbed the doorknob of the swinging door and entered the room. At this point, our dogs were howling and whimpering outside. Inside the room, a man's deep voice recited obscenities. The priest spread holy water in every corner of the room simultaneously. The ritual seemed to be at its peak, and just when I thought I couldn't bear it another moment, everything ceased.

After the purification of our house, the odd noises and haunting occurrences seemed to end. At least we hoped they did. Today, approximately forty-five years later, continuous paranormal incidents have occurred in that house.

It has been reported that sounds of a radio will play when a person approaches the house, even though there is no electricity hooked up. Others have heard banging coming from within the house as well as a man screaming. Several photographs have captured a woman dressed in turn-of-the-twentieth-century clothes on the porch and in the front windows. Some have claimed to hear a deep growling noise from the front yard. Several pictures have captured up to ten floating faces on the front porch and a shadow creature in a hooded cloak on the street in front of the house.

The exorcism may have calmed the spirits, but it did not close the vortex located at the heart of the house. My mother may have unknowingly left the opening to the other side by not correctly sealing the vortex opened by the Ouija board and making this spirit-laden home the most haunted house in Bisbee.

BISBEE FIRE STATION NO. 2

This fire station stands almost directly in the middle of Tombstone Canyon Road, about one mile from Highway 80. After 1910, Upper Tombstone Canyon was expanding and considered to be one of the "nicer parts of town." More than one thousand houses had sprung up, and the citizens were demanding their own fire station by 1914. Surprisingly, some members of the city council were opposed to another firehouse, saying there was not enough fresh water or drainage and that the property was flood prone. Eventually, the council voted to buy the property for the new fire station. The building was completed on September 30, 1914, and modernized in 1993.

The plans for the building included a two-story structure, all concrete, with living quarters for the firemen upstairs and a pole for a fast slide down to the main floor, where the horses and wagons were kept.

Bisbee Fire Department history includes the first volunteer fire department, created on October 1, 1894. The headquarters was located on Main Street, across from where the Bisbee Restoration Museum and Café ROKA stand now. In 1898, a brick structure was built on the north side of the same street as the new headquarters. A bell on top of the building sounded the alert in the case of fires. It was located next to where the Bank of Bisbee building is today. The volunteer crew depended on a natural water supply and a bucket brigade.

In later years, there was also a firehouse on Naco Road, near the entrance to what is now Old Bisbee. But the route from there to upper Tombstone Canyon was very curvy, not conducive for the horse-drawn fire wagons used at that time, and the location didn't sit well with residents up the canyon.

In May 2008, the Bisbee Fire Department celebrated one hundred years as Arizona's first full-time paid crew. In October of the same year, Bisbee had the worst disaster in its history. A fire destroyed almost the entire Main Street. Property valued at nearly $750,000 in the business section of town and $3,000 worth of residential property was destroyed. This was the largest fire ever recorded there.

On June 29, 1909, the Bisbee Fire Department was called to put out a fire in a boxcar where several bottles of hydrochloric acid had broken and started a fire. A firefighter named George Marz began to move the containers after the firemen thought they had completely extinguished the blaze. Suddenly, flames flared up, and with them the acid fumes. Marz inhaled those deadly vapors and became seriously ill the next day.

His brother Joe Marz showed up at the firehouse and talked George into coming home with him and his wife. A doctor was called and reported to his family that George was in very bad condition. The next morning, George said he was feeling better, but by noon he had lost consciousness. He died at 7:00 p.m. that night. His death certificate reports that he died on July 1, 1909, due to edema of the lungs, the result of inhaling acid fumes. He is the only Bisbee fireman to lose his life in the line of duty.

Back to Fire Station No. 2. As you enter the front door, you come into the garage. The first things you see are a firetruck and an emergency vehicle. There is also the original fire pole still intact to your left. Before the renovation, the entire upstairs living quarters were completely switched around. The sleeping area was in the front and open with beds lined in rows. The kitchen and recreation area were in the back.

There are two firefighters assigned to each three-day shift at No. 2. The modernization of the building was designed for more people in the future and for other crews during emergency situations, such as wildfire crews. There is a "firehose dryer" in front of the building—the only one of its kind. It is in front of the building and above an approximately fifteen-foot-deep ditch. In the early 1970s, firemen built the structure.

For several years, a rumor circulated around Bisbee that Fire Station No. 2 was haunted. I used to be the editor in chief of our family-owned online paranormal magazine, *Spirits of Cochise County*. I organized a "ghost hunt" to see if the rumor was true. Our ghost hunt, the first at the station, took place in 2009. Members of Spirits of Cochise County Investigators (SCCI) tackled that story and set out to see if it was true.

A former firefighter who had died of a mysterious gunshot wound while at home is the resident ghost. At first, he was thought to have committed suicide, but later, according to interviews with retired Bisbee firefighters, the case was changed to an accidental death. The fireman lived close to the station. When he did not show up for work, his coworker went looking for him at his house and found him dead. The now-retired firefighter said he thinks his friend is haunting the historic building with several activities resembling practical jokes over the years. He told me that the deceased fireman always said that if he died, he would come back and haunt the station.

Generations of firefighters have had numerous paranormal experiences and express them openly. They also use the resident ghost as part of their initiation of the "new guy" on shift. They'll leave the new firefighter alone in the building or assign him or her to lock up on their own.

Ghostly activity includes doors down the hall to the bedrooms opening after they have been locked at night and the shower in the upstairs quarters of the station turning on by itself. Numerous witnesses have seen wet footprints along the hallway, leading away from the bathroom. Pots and pans jangle on their own. The apparition of a fireman in different areas of the building is often seen. Witnesses say they have seen an apparition walk straight through a wall near the kitchen!

Footsteps are heard coming up the steep stairs to the second level when nobody is there. Phantasmal sounds of "tinkering around" downstairs at the tool bench near the firetrucks is a common occurrence at the station. Firefighters have also reported feeling their hands or arms being touched, as to wake them while they sleep, and the feeling of being held down while they sleep.

For the duration of our paranormal investigation, a few emergency calls blared through the building. When the second call came in, we caught a chilling electronic voice phenomenon (EVP) of an eerie voice responding to a medical emergency call. During the actual radio correspondence, a male voice belonging to emergency personnel asked a female voice if she needed assistance. The female voice responded. Almost instantly, a disembodied voice responded with, "moving…."

If this is the voice of a firefighter from days gone by, he seems to still be on duty. He's listening to conversations in the firehouse and hovers over each bed, making sure his comrades are resting before the next emergency interrupts their sleep.

After the paranormal investigation, I asked the ghost to play a prank when I left on the two firefighters who had given us a tour of the building. I was told later that when my team left the building and the firefighters came back into the main firehouse, a light bulb burst and made a loud noise. The firemen said they laughed and made sure I got the message that the ghost obliged my request for a good prank.

While I was giving a haunted tour of the fire station in 2016, on the cement bridge over a deep ditch and directly in front of the building, a woman was listening to me and decided to try to sit on the bridge's pipe

Haunted Bisbee Fire Station and "hose drying rack," where a resident ghost saved a tour guest from falling over and into the deep ditch below.

fence. She said that she could not maintain her balance and exclaimed to everyone that "someone" had grabbed her arm and pushed her off the fence onto solid ground. She said it was the dead fireman! "He saved me from falling down into the ditch!" She added, "He saved my life!"

COCHISE COUNTY SUPERIOR COURT—BISBEE COURTHOUSE

Numerous historical newspaper articles and books report that there was a very heated Cochise County election on November 19, 1929. On that fall day, it was decided that the county seat would be moved from Tombstone to Bisbee. By December 1, the Cochise County Board of Supervisors picked the location for the new courthouse on Higgins Hill, off Tombstone Canyon Road. Bonds in the amount of $300,000 were approved on

The Cochise County Courthouse was completed in 1931, after it was decided in 1929 to move the county seat from Tombstone to Bisbee.

February 25, 1930, for the construction of the Pueblo Deco building. It would be for the courts and offices of county officials, and a jail would be built on the site.

The total cost of the build was $250,000, and it was finished by 1931. The architect was Roy Place from Tucson; the Clinton Campbell Construction Company, from Phoenix, was the contractor. A dedication of the building was made on August 3, 1931, by Arizona governor George W.P. Hunt.

There are many remarkable things about the courthouse. The roof is copper-plated, and the front doors to the lobby are made of bronze. The lobby is trimmed with Belgian black marble on the base and paneled with Tennessee pink marble. The wood trim throughout the courthouse is mahogany. The copper bird fountain in the front of the building was made at the Copper Queen Reduction Works in Douglas and, in recent years, was renovated by the local bar association. The front steps leading to the building are made of silica and granite arch stone, made from arroyo sand from the Fike Ranch at Naco, Arizona.

The old jail from the Tombstone courthouse was removed and placed in the new building. The third floor was originally the county jail and included a dormitory for attendants and trustees. Four cellblocks accommodated a total of sixty-five prisoners. On the fourth floor was the jail for eight women and four female juveniles. On the fifth floor was a jury dormitory.

On July 3, 1980, this courthouse was listed in the National Register of Historic Places. The new county jail was built in 1985 with 160 cells. That jail is located on Highway 80, on the outskirts of Bisbee.

At the turn of the millennium, I was working at the Bisbee Courthouse as a clerk. Within days of beginning working there, I started experiencing odd phenomena. One morning, I was having a conversation with a security guard named Hector. We discussed the many eerie noises and sensations the building seemed to produce.

I told him about hearing footsteps upstairs in the lobby when no one else was around and being completely creeped out when I had to go upstairs and look for court files in the old jail. And I said that when I went downstairs for different files, where the sheriff's department used to be located, I saw an apparition of a women dashing right by me.

He told me about his own experiences, how he had heard similar noises during different shifts and how, at random times, the courthouse doors would slam shut on their own. He said other employees confessed to hearing several voices speaking when he or other employees came in for work when the building was empty.

The odd noises and creepy voices may be part of a residual haunting—a memory with a thick string lingering from the past attached to a building filled with erupting emotions.

The female entity I saw in the old sheriff's office isn't the only ghost too stubborn to leave the courthouse. The other ghost has been seen by many and seen well enough to compare him to his picture hanging in the same building. His name is John Wilson Ross. He was born in November 1863 in Berryville, Arkansas, and was the youngest of a family of eight children. He traveled to Flagstaff in 1888 and taught school at Camp Verde. He later began practicing law in Flagstaff, Prescott and Jerome before arriving in Bisbee. He was the first Cochise County superior judge at the new courthouse. He served there from 1931 to 1942, when he was defeated in the 1942 Democratic primary by Frank E. Thomas. He died on June 30, 1945, in Pueblo, Colorado, at the age of eighty-one.

Judge Ross was a very significant and prominent Bisbee resident. He ran as a Republican candidate for superior court judge at Tombstone in 1911, but by 1914, he was holding meetings for the Progressive Party at his office, located in the Medigovich Hall building in Bisbee. He was considered one of the leading lawyers in Arizona and was on many committees and councils.

In the spring of 1918, the judge held a well-attended meeting at the City Park to organize the circulation of the petitions for nominating the city as a candidate for the courthouse. By November of that year, while working as a Cochise County attorney, he had accepted the position of associate justice of the Supreme Court of Arizona. He was the brother of Henry D. Ross, who at the time was already a member of the state supreme court.

Judge John Ross's wife, Lida Norris Ross, was also involved with the community and was a member of Bisbee's socialite circle. They shared a

The county courthouse eerily looks over Tombstone Canyon Road below. An art deco beauty in the daylight, it is chillingly haunting at night!

lovely, brick-veneered home on Shattuck Street in the Warren District. Lida Ross died on January 19, 1923.

The apparition of Judge Ross has been seen in the Division 2 courtroom and the judge's chambers along with the smell of a cigar or a cigarette. He has also been seen in the second-floor lobby. Witnesses have reported that they have seen him walk from the judge's bench back to his chambers. The judge also shows himself in the old jail on the top floors of the courthouse.

A custodian reported that as she was mopping at the foot of the stairway in front of the main entrance of the courthouse and facing the doors, she felt as if someone was looking at her. The feeling was so intense that she had to stop mopping and instinctively turned around and looked up to the small mezzanine of the stairway.

A man dressed in a 1940s-era three-piece suit was staring down at her. The county worker was taken aback and said that the man had wire glasses. The worker said he had "crazy eyes." The custodian looked down for a moment, and when she looked up toward the steps again, the apparition had vanished.

All these years after his death, his robust and dominating presence is still felt by many who are brought to this place to be held accountable for their actions or to be acquitted of any charges. Nevertheless, Judge John W. Ross will be witness to their fate and will, in his own way, make sure the beauty and justice of his courthouse are being preserved.

LORETTO SCHOOL AND THE COFFEE NUN

The Loretto Academy was Bisbee's Roman Catholic convent school on Higgins Hill behind and to the side of the Bisbee Courthouse. The school is only a few feet from the town's fourth Catholic church and Bisbee's second St. Patrick's Church. The first Catholic church (1884–90) was a small cabin near Naco Road. This was the first organized church in the mining camp. A larger, adobe building located on Quality Hill was the second Catholic church. As the town grew, so did the congregation. In 1891, enough funds were raised, and a new building was constructed at School Hill on Clawson Avenue. It was named St. Patrick's. By 1896, a rectory had been built for a priest who shared his time in Bisbee and Tombstone.

St. Patrick's was a segregated congregation at the time. More than four thousand members who were Mexican American and Mexican nationals were able to build a Catholic church of their own. They erected the building on Chihuahua Hill, which sits high above Brewery Gulch. Because of the two separate churches, there had to be two priests.

Father Winard Meurer came to take over the Anglo-American parish in 1905 and soon realized the need for a Catholic school. Thomas Higgins, who at this point had moved to Los Angeles, was a very prominent Bisbee miner and owner of many valuable mines in Bisbee. He donated a parcel of the surface land of his mining claim, called the Aurora. As soon as he heard about the school, he decided to help.

Fundraising was very successful, and enough money was collected for the construction of the academy. By 1907, a Mission Revival–style, three-story building was finished. It was originally named the Loretto Academy and served kindergarten through the twelfth grade, run by the Loretto nuns; by 1910, it had two hundred students. The school was designed by Henry Trost.

The Loretto Academy was not segregated, as the two parishes were, and it did allow students of both ethnic backgrounds to attend. It was later renamed St. Patrick's School and closed its doors in the early 1970s.

For decades, the downstairs bathrooms have had a reputation as a spooky place often avoided by students. Children have claimed that they have seen an apparition of an elderly nun who may have lived in the local

Loretto Academy in picturesque Bisbee. A Catholic school run by the Sisters of Loretto, it is now haunted by a nun who refuses to leave.

abbey. It has been seen on the bottom floor and where bathrooms are located, wearing the black floor-length gown and habit traditionally worn by Catholic nuns years ago.

A clue that it is near is when a strong aroma of coffee arises. The ghost will also turn on the water faucets of the bathroom when someone enters. It will show itself in the mirrors as it dashes past and behind the handwasher, causing a light breeze.

For many years, the Loretto sisters were housed in a large building on Taylor Avenue near Central School, but they were eventually moved to a large, more modern home right across from the academy. The woman who haunts the old and now empty school most likely lived on Taylor Avenue.

Why would such a religious person linger in this world as a supernatural entity? It is a great mystery. She may have been quite content in the role of teacher and so continues to monitor and keep order, making sure all children wash their hands and seeing to it that there is no running in the halls.

2
MAIN STREET

THE BISBEE MASSACRE

Bisbee's Main Street in 1883 was a long and very narrow dirt road with perhaps just enough room for two wagons to pass each other—about eighteen feet wide. Buildings on the street were made mostly of wood and were tightly fitted on either side of the street. Letson Block is where two buildings recorded as the oldest on Main Street were located and the site of the Bisbee Massacre.

In 1888, James Letson built the Mansion House Hotel, an adobe building on the left. On the right, he built the Turf Saloon in 1894. Before the Letson Block was built, in the same location stood the Goldwater-Castañeda Store.

The Bon Ton Saloon was next to the Letson Hotel, in front of what is now 28 Main Street. The Goldwater-Castañeda Store is where 22 and 24 Main Street are today. Across the street is where the Hardy's Store used to stand (23 Main Street). The owner left town suddenly, leaving the store vacant for a man named John Heath. He opened a dance hall there, according to James F. Duncan of Tombstone, a witness. Some historians say his dance hall was not on that spot but at 38 Main. At today's 29 Main, Annie Roberts owned a restaurant that was adjoined to two saloons. Bill Daniels owned one, and William Roberts owned the other.

On the snowy night of December 8, 1883, four people, plus an unborn child, were murdered on Main Street in Bisbee. They were shot and killed by a gang of bandits robbing the only safe in town and what they thought would be $7,000 in payroll money.

During the first week of December, five strangers were seen loitering around town, keeping a low profile. At 7:00 p.m. on December 8, these same five men rode up Mule Gulch with old bandanas covering their faces. They passed the smelter and dismounted their horses at Preston's Lumberyard near where the library and post office are today. From there, they made their way to the Goldwater-Castañeda Store on the same side of the street.

Two of the men, Dan Dowd and Billy Delaney, stationed themselves on the sidewalk at the entrance to the store. There was a delivery wagon parked in front. Dan Kelly, Red Sample and Tex Howard entered the store. As soon as those men entered, they yelled for everyone inside to raise their hands in the air.

José Miguel Castañeda, the store manager, was at the back of the store near a bedroom door. Thinking fast, he grabbed several hundred dollars and went into the back room. He placed the money under the pillow and lay down on a bed and faked being sick. Tex Howard followed him and screamed and pushed at him to get up, then took his cash and shoved Castañeda back into the store.

In the meantime, Red Sample had Joe Goldwater open the safe. Sample told Goldwater, "Get the payroll."

Goldwater answered, "That's where you're fooled. The stagecoach is late. The money is not here."

Sample pushed Goldwater aside and helped himself to some Mexican money and some valuables belonging to several Bisbee residents.

Outside, two Bisbee men, John Tappiner and Joseph Bright, came out of the Bon Ton Saloon and started to go past Dowd and Delaney as they walked up the street. Delaney commanded the two men to go into the store. Tappiner said he would not and turned to go back into the saloon. Bright started to run up the street with Dowd firing after him.

Delaney's first shot missed Tappiner, but the second shot hit him in the head, tearing away a portion of his skull and leaving the brains running off the porch of the Bon Ton Saloon, where he fell.

While this was happening, a volunteer fireman named James Krigbaum and some others ran out of the alley between where the Western Bank building and 5 Main are now and started shooting at the bandits. Krigbaum took aim at one of the tall outlaws, only grazing his coat.

Next to the Goldwater-Castañeda Store was Joe Mary's Saloon, where a man named Howard stepped out and was gunned down instantly. This spot is now in front of 18 and 20 Main Street.

At this time, a deputy from New Mexico named Tom Smith was with his wife eating supper in Sima's Restaurant (25 Main Street). Deputy Smith came out and ordered them to quit shooting and told them he was a lawman. Delaney told him, "You're the man we're lookin' for." He then shot Smith in the left shoulder.

Deputy Smith remarked, "I am hit."

Delaney said, "I will give you another."

The second shot killed Smith. The deputy's body was found between the shafts of the delivery wagon. After being shot the second time, he had crawled through from the back of the wagon and died.

The story of the next victim is a shocking and sad one. A pregnant Annie Roberts was standing at the door of her restaurant (29 Main Street) when the shooting began. She came to take a peek to see what was causing the commotion outside. When she turned to go back into the building, one of the balls from Dowd's gun missed Bright and passed through the doorjamb, lodging in the small of her back. Roberts died in terrible agony the next morning.

J.A. Nolly was in a saloon (21 Main) when the shooting started. He ran out and was shot by Dowd in the belly. Nolly died the following week.

After that, the gang managed to get out of town while two Bisbee men, Bill Daniels and John Reynolds, ran down the gulch with guns blazing, chasing the bandits. They didn't manage to hit a target. The shooting of the Bisbee Massacre lasted a total of about fifteen minutes.

Immediately, Krigbaum was sent to Tombstone. The *Bisbee Review* said he made it there on his horse in about two hours. Ironically, on the way, he passed the stagecoach with the $7,000 the gang was after.

A posse was organized the same night with forty-five to fifty men. Daniels and a man named John Heath were part of the search party. When the posse reached a fork in the road at Forest Ranch, Heath tried to convince the others that the gang must be heading north toward the Dragoons or even Tombstone. The others disagreed strongly with Heath's opinion and headed toward Sulphur Springs Valley and the Chiricahua Mountains instead. Heath went north.

The posse was on the gang's trail, which led them to the ranch of Dan Ross. Near the Ross house was a large crevice in the rock, twenty to twenty-five feet deep. Here the posse found the carcasses of horses. They had been run almost to death. The bandits stripped them of their bridles and saddles and brutally shoved them into the crevice, leaving them there to die. They then walked, carrying their saddles and bridles, into the ranch of Frank Buckles, where they camped for several days before stealing his horses.

After that appalling discovery, the posse continued its trek and stopped at the cabin of Luben Pardu. Pardu said that five men had stopped at his place and had divided up some money and items, then left in different directions. He also said that another man and the same group had been at his cabin a week before. The other man seemed to act like the leader of the group. He named all five men, plus John Heath as their leader. Heath was quickly found in Bisbee and taken to Tombstone.

Eventually, months later, the men were caught. On February 8, 1884, the defendants were brought into court to make their pleas. Each pleaded not guilty. Heath was tried alone. On February 17, at 8:00 p.m., the jurors gave Heath the verdict of guilty of murder in the second degree. On February 21, he was sentenced to life imprisonment.

A large group of Bisbee citizens were worried that he would live long enough to be pardoned. They decided to take the law into their own hands, to avoid the possibility that Heath would take his case to the U.S. Supreme Court.

A committee of safety, called "45/60," announced that "John Heath was guilty as hell and deserved the same punishment as the others."

On the morning of February 22, 1884, the committee, made up of some of the most influential Bisbee citizens, traveled to Tombstone and, at 8:00 a.m., marched to the jail unmasked. Two men kicked at the jail's gate, and chief jailer Billy Ward opened the door on their demand. The jailer was expecting breakfast for the prisoners at that time and answered unarmed. They ordered him to give up, then unlocked the cell.

They grabbed Heath, and a rope held by several men was placed around his waist. They dragged the man and ran down Toughnut Street to a point below where the railroad crosses the street. The rope was then hung to a telegraph pole.

Witnesses say that Heath coolly pulled a handkerchief from his pocket and folded it, then a person covered his eyes with it. Heath asked the crowd not to fill his body with lead, and they told him they wouldn't.

In an instant, he was strung up. His body hung there for many hours before he was taken down and sent to the county physician's office of Dr. George Goodfellow. Heath's death certificate reads, "John Heath came to his death from emphysema of the lungs, a disease common in high altitudes, which might have been caused by strangulation, self-inflicted or otherwise."

On February 19, 1884, the five bandits were sentenced for the murders. On March 25, each was hanged by the neck until dead.

John Heath hangs from a telegraph pole in Tombstone on February 22, 1884, after a Bisbee mob dragged him from jail and hanged him.

The graves of Heath and the five members of the gang are in the Boothill Cemetery in Tombstone.

Main Street today is different than it was back in 1883. All of the buildings were made of wood but now are made of brick, adobe or cement. Of course, the street is paved, and because of the buildings and their proximity, sound bounces very well, with lots of echo.

In the evening hours, and especially when the road seems silent, a plague of sadness can overwhelm you as you stroll past each of the sites where innocent people were gunned down. In front of the old F.W. Woolworth Company's variety store building there have been reports of a woman's low bellowing cry in the earliest morning hours. Along with that sound comes a young man's voice calling out inaudible words to her. It seems that the female voice ignores his and continues to weep, causing echoes of misery along the narrow street.

With such a degree of pain and suffering as a result of the massacre, it is not surprising to hear phantasmal cries and to see dark shadows forming and disappearing on Main Street. The eerie noises are best heard in the wee hours of the night.

Heath's grave site at Boothill in Tombstone, Arizona.

Bisbee's Main Street will likely be one of the most fascinating and gorgeous roads in Arizona for years to come, regardless of the event that took place there well over one hundred years ago.

BISBEE RESTORATION MUSEUM

At 37 Main Street, a gorgeous three-story building with a large basement stands with original signage cemented above the doorway. This building used to be the location of the Fair store and is now home to the Bisbee Restoration Museum.

The original building was severely damaged during the Great 1908 Bisbee Fire. In fact, one of the Fair store owners, Sam Frankenberg, was among the first witnesses of the fire, which started at the original Grand Hotel, only a few doorways up the street. An estimated $300,000 in stock and warehouse goods were lost at the store, as well as the building itself. A grand opening of the new store took place in November 1909.

In 1913, Bisbee's Main Street was considered a modern business thoroughfare. It was estimated that millions of dollars were invested in capital and mercantile stocks. The *Bisbee Daily Review* reported that, in that business block, more money was represented than in any other in the entire Southwest.

Sam's brother Ben Frankenberg began the Fair store in a tiny room on Brewery Avenue. Only fifteen by twenty square feet, the business soon outgrew the space. Ben moved into the large structure then known as the Costello building on Main Street.

Success was always in the cards for the Fair store; it expanded beyond the space of that building, too. In the last month of 1900, the brothers took over more space of the building, giving them ample sections for various departments. Not only did they have more room for displays, but they also had the large thirty-six-by-eighty-square-foot warehouse room that was constantly being depleted then refilled with merchandise. This was located on Subway Street and had a breezeway extending from the second story. By 1901, it was owned and run by the firm Frankenberg Bros. and Newman.

For staff, Ben Frankenberg had extraordinary talent from across the country, individuals who had previously been employed at establishments in New York City, Chicago and Detroit. The store's departments were elegant and high-end. The Fair store policy was one of "come and see," as it had a tremendous reputation for glorious displays of merchandise in all departments.

The store had a selection of clothing, hats and shoes for women, men and children. Sam managed the men's department and carpets. He would go on three-week excursions to Chicago and New York to find the finest material

The Fair store, now the Bisbee Restoration Museum, is elegantly located on a curve on Main Street.

for sewing and the latest fashions for clothing, hats and shoes. Ben would go on the same type of trips as well.

As the years went by, the Fair store kept up with the times. At one point, it had a whole slew of seamstresses and tailors for all customers. They wanted to make sure everyone was custom-fitted and satisfied with their purchases.

The owners of the Fair were respected in the community and of high stature in society. Keeping up with the reputation of being fair went a long way for the business and for the individuals who ran it until 1928. After that, the building housed various types of businesses. It was a women's clothing store, a dry-goods store and a Western Auto Store. By 1968, the building had been donated by the Frankenberg and Newman families to the Restoration Council of Bisbee and instantly turned into the museum it is today.

It is an extraordinary place, full of donated items from people with ties to Bisbee. It is called the "people's museum," as it displays how people have lived in the mining town from when it was a camp to present times. All of the staff serve on a volunteer basis, and the museum is a 501(c)(3) nonprofit organization with a donation entry fee.

During the time of my tour business, I was able to ghost hunt in various Bisbee buildings. The Fair store building was one of them. I worked closely with the volunteers at the Bisbee Restoration Museum and learned from a couple of volunteers that there was a resident ghost and that it had shown itself on different occasions. A volunteer said that she had seen an apparition of a woman on the second floor. Another staff member said that she heard various noises on the same floor and sometimes near the sewing machines, at times when she knew she was the only person in the building. She also stated that she heard a phantom-type woman's voice saying something faintly, many times after she unlocked the front door before the museum opened.

On my birthday a few years ago, three of us, after hours and at night, were able to meet and seek out the ghost at the museum. This was an investigation before a paranormal event, in collaboration with the museum, to be held later that month, which included three successful séances. During our ghost hunt, we took several photos, and as we went, I made recordings. At times, a disembodied female voice was recorded.

We settled down on the large mezzanine between the first and second floors, sitting on some chairs with the lights off. We began to ask the resident ghost a slew of questions. We then asked her to tap somewhere in the building to answer "yes." She did, near the antique sewing machines displayed in the museum.

We told her we would recite the alphabet and asked her to tap when we got to the letters in her name. By the end of that session, she communicated "Elaina." "Did you work in the Fair store?" She tapped. She offered no response to having the position of a shop girl, clerk or saleslady but indicated "yes" to a seamstress. We asked her if she recognized the individuals there that night. She tapped "yes" to the staff members but "no" to me.

We asked if the ghost knew Ben Frankenberg, and she said "yes." She also said she was not alone in the building. She said a son was with her. Through more questions, we understood that she was in her thirties and had brought her young son to work, which made her happy. She also confessed that, in present times, her son moves things around in the museum as a way of playing some sort of game with members of the staff.

We stopped asking questions, because we didn't seem to get many more responses. Spirits who communicate with the living get tired quickly. As we sat in silence, suddenly, quick, short steps went from one side of the second floor above us to the other. The sound was coming from hard-soled shoes in petite strides. I whispered loudly and said to the others, "Do you hear that?" They nodded that they did. That was the last oddity that took place that evening.

During the three séances I held at the museum, the female ghost kindly obliged and made herself known to several people attending the three-day event. When I asked her to make noises to respond to my several questions and questions asked by tour guests, noises were heard near the sewing machines on the second floor where we were set up. Several guests and I said we heard her footsteps around the large room as we continued the event. She was a highly active ghost, and it was an incredible experience to bear witness to it.

If you have the fortune of visiting the Bisbee Restoration Museum on Bisbee's Main Street, you might run into a young seamstress from a time when Bisbee was at its finest and run into a little boy who may be lurking behind a counter, ready to play a game of hide-and-seek.

Bisbee Daily Review Building

The Copper Queen Dispensary was built in 1898 on the site where the *Bisbee Daily Review* is now on Main Street. Here, single men were treated for minor injuries and illnesses, while women and children were treated at home.

Bisbee, until it was incorporated as a city, had horrendous sanitary conditions. Residents had to contend with smallpox, typhoid fever and other sicknesses and diseases. The dust clung to the streets and inside homes; during monsoon season, the same streets were turned into marshes.

A big problem was that drinking water was taken from shallow wells, causing a typhoid epidemic, which took the lives of hundreds of people in just two years, from 1888 to 1890. It took that long before it was understood that it was coming from contaminated spring water.

Dr. James Douglas of Phelps Dodge fame felt responsible for the well-being of the miners and their families in Bisbee. Since many came to the area for a job in one of his many prosperous mines, he in turn took it upon himself to hold lectures and demonstrations to make the residents understand the importance of sanitation.

The other mining corporations in town seemed to have the same attitude, not only regarding the sanitation situation but also the many accidents that took place while mining. They began to build hospitals around the town. Now emergency medical care was given to miners injured on the job, and their family members were able to receive medications and care. Of course, a miner had to pay a monthly fee for the healthcare given at the dispensary.

In 1907, the old dispensary was partially torn down and the front extended to be in line with the new library building. The staff at the dispensary on Main Street moved into the new Copper Queen Hospital in 1914. The *Bisbee Review* moved into the building in 1915. Back in 1909, Phelps Dodge Corporation began to buy all the mining district papers that William Kelly, the owner, was running. By 1925, they owned all of them, including the *Bisbee Daily Review*.

Phelps Dodge Corporation wanted to make sure "that nothing reflecting unfavorably on the company would appear in newsprint."

A well-seasoned newspaperman named Bill Epler bought the *Bisbee Daily Review* from Phelps Dodge in 1971 and sold it in 1974 to the Wick family. Epler had changed the paper into a weekly publication; in 1976, Walt and Milton Wick once again published it daily. This is when they merged the *Sierra Vista Herald* with the *Bisbee Daily Review*.

In the summer of 1981, a Sunday edition was introduced. As of 2004, the paper was a seven-day, morning newspaper. The *Sierra Vista Herald* and the *Bisbee Daily Review* are published out of Sierra Vista, Arizona.

A traumatic incident took place at the building on October 2, 1905. A Copper Queen Store employee died at the dispensary. It was reported that a fatal cough ended the life of Frank Cory in a dramatic fashion, on Main Street.

Cory had initially rushed into the library next door. He charged into the reading room and asked J.J. Scott to please call him a doctor. Scott instantly grabbed at Cory, who quickly collapsed into his arms. The

"The Review" sign flags the building where the *Bisbee Daily Review* has made its home since 1915.

The *Bisbee Daily Review* building today. It was the Copper Queen Dispensary from 1898 to 1914. Here, Frank Cory died a frantic death.

unconscious man was carried into the Copper Queen Dispensary, suffering from hemorrhaging of the lungs and unconscious from the loss of blood.

The pharmacist, Mr. Hunter, immediately called Dr. Hagan, who was in the back of the building with another patient. The doctor ran to Cory and began to administer medications. The patient initially responded well, but when Dr. Hagan tried to give him ice, Cory was seized with a severe fit of coughing, making it impossible to retain the ice in his mouth. All the while, blood was seeping from his mouth.

The doctor tried other meds, but the man did not respond and died in twenty minutes. It was quite a chaotic scene on the street, as people were running from the library to see what was happening to Cory.

Judge Owen Murphy and Deputy Sheriff Biddy Doyle were called to examine the body of Cory and found his name written on his undershirt. Sixty-nine dollars was found in his pockets; later, at the mortuary, an additional forty dollars was found sewn somewhere in his pants. The investigators found out that Cory had been employed in the grocery department of the Copper Queen Store and was in the last stages of tuberculosis, with a large cavity in his left lung.

A close friend of Cory's said the grocery clerk had just resigned the day before so that he could leave for Panama the next day to take a position with the government there, thinking he would feel better and recover from his illness.

This was only one of the many dramatic situations that took place at the dispensary. There have been reports of paranormal activity in the old building. A person testified that in the back, in the early morning, they can hear footsteps pacing back and forth when no one else is in the building. Sometimes, the pacing sounds more aggressive, as if running instead of walking.

An ex-employee of the newspaper office confided to me that they have seen shadows that cross a back window when no one is in the room and have heard creaking on the old floors at places when there is no one standing or walking.

3

OK Street and
Youngblood Hill

OK Street is a unique road that is very narrow and runs directly above Brewery Gulch, with an extreme decline at Youngblood Hill Avenue—or incline, if you're traveling in the other direction. The road used to be called OK Train and OK Trail. The road is located on Chihuahua Hill and was renamed OK Street shortly after a major fire in 1907, becoming part of the fire district.

Two Bisbee pioneers, brothers Henry and Frank Dubacher, were the first to be in that area. They built their house and corral there. The Dubacher brothers were born in Lucerne, Switzerland, and arrived in Bisbee in 1879. They had been in Tombstone prospecting and traveled over the Mule Mountains. When they came into Bisbee, they met the only other white men in the mining camp and decided to bunk with them. They camped in a nearby canyon thick with trees and perfect for lumber. That area is now affectionally called "Dubacher Canyon."

They immediately got themselves into the wood-supplying business, meeting the needs of the new mining district. But they didn't do that too long. They took a chance on the brewery business.

Youngblood Hill Avenue is an extreme sloped road positioned between Brewery Avenue and OK Street. It has a drainage channel that runs the length of the avenue. The Works Progress Administration (WPA) most likely built the channel during its 1938 campaign in Bisbee.

Left: OK Street with the Philadelphia Hotel and turret of the Pythian Castle. Both are creations of Joseph Muheim Sr. and other prominent Bisbee pioneers.

Right: Youngblood Hill's extreme slant is a two-way street that leads from OK Street to Brewery Avenue. In the middle of the road stands the Muheim Heritage House Museum.

COUNTY BRANCH JAIL/OK STREET JAILHOUSE

Bisbee's history of county and city jails in the earliest days is covered in scandal and disgust. The first city jail is thought to have been located near the south side of Main Street just above Subway Street. It was continuously being criticized by the press, described as a single eight-by-eight-foot cage that at times confined six or seven drunk men. "The Bisbee Jail is a disgrace," stated the *Tombstone Epitaph* in 1892. It added that immediate action to clean it up must be taken by government leaders.

Over on OK Street, the county branch jail wasn't much better. The jail was overcrowded, unventilated and filthy. Jailbreaks and rebellious acts of violence were common at both facilities. In February 1902, at the county jail, two people walking by saw a thick cloud of black smoke flowing through the building's front door and alerted authorities. A prisoner had set fire to a mattress in response to the conditions.

The surrounding newspapers and a committee of the city council and Bisbee Women's Club brought attention to the situation. They pressured

Originally built as the Cochise County Branch Jail in 1905, this building is now haunted by ghosts serving a much longer sentence than expected.

the city council and the Cochise County Board of Supervisors to build better facilities. The city jail did undergo improvements in 1903, but it was abandoned and closed around 1907.

A reporter from the *Bisbee Daily Review* was put on assignment to investigate the situation at the county branch jail on OK Street. County officials gave the reporter the chance to obtain a personal inspection by locking him up for several hours. In the May 18, 1904 issue of the newspaper, that same unnamed journalist, because of his firsthand experience, was able to write a front-page exposé that enlightened the community and the county of the conditions.

He called the jail an abominable nuisance and a filth hole beyond power of any pen to describe. But he gave it a good try, writing, "The 'Black Hole' of Calcutta is a Garden of Eden in comparison with this place they call jail."

He described the overcrowded conditions of twenty people in two little rooms and a hall. There was absolutely no ventilation, and the inmates breathed recycled foul air. He witnessed that the men were dressed only in trousers. He described the building as incredibly hot and creeping and crawling with vermin, which had no means of escape in the location he called a hellhole creation. Apparently, sheet iron was nailed over the door, blocking any fresh air from coming in or bad air going out.

He also said the place was a disease-breeding joint, an uncivilized and barbaric hotel that the county was maintaining in the very midst of the city of Bisbee.

Cochise County supervisor Thomas York agreed with all who were outraged with the standard of the county jail. Because Bisbee was one of the heaviest contributors of taxes, as well as its income and increasing population, it deserved a commendable building. He advised for a healthy budget of $20,000 toward a new jail and recommended an addition of a kitchen to the premises and hiring a "competent" jailer for a twenty-four-hour shift.

During an epic city council meeting on May 4, 1904, the same committee from the council and the Bisbee Women's Club gave a report of their investigation of the county branch jail. A member said about the facility that it was "not fit to put a dog in."

The city council agreed and declared it a public nuisance and gave a direct message to the county that if the jail wasn't cleaned at once, it would be condemned and ordered to be torn down. The county complied and fumigated and cleaned out the jail and cut out windows, exposing the infestation of an array of insects and rodents, which scurried into cracks and holes in the walls and floors.

It was decided that the county jail was too far gone to save. With a push from Supervisor York, the county went beyond just tidying up the facility. The "Black Hole of Bisbee" was to be torn down. In the meantime, prisoners were to be moved to the city jail at once, even before advertisements for bids on building the new one were published in the newspapers.

A *Bisbee Daily Review* article, "Down Comes the Filthy Vermin Infested Jail," noted, "While the new jail is being built, the proper precautions will be made to have the prisoners cleaned and disinfected from head to foot, before placing them in the city jail." There was a push to have the new county branch jail built within sixty days of the teardown.

Cochise County supervisors ordered the county clerk to advertise in the *Tombstone Prospector*, *Bisbee Daily Review* and *Douglas International* for architects and bids for the construction of the new jail, which was to be erected on the same site as the old one. A "Notice to Architects" was published daily through most of the summer of 1904 with a plan and specifications for a two-story county branch jail. It would have six steel cells on the second floor made of concrete and supported by steel beams. The first floor would have a jailer's room and hall. The budget for construction was $12,000. In addition, the jail would be equipped with electric lights and toilets.

Two completely different obstacles arose and delayed the building's construction. A very influential Bisbee man named Baptiste Caretto claimed in July 1904 that the excavation for the foundation of the jail extended to his private property and would block off an old public trail. He proposed to board of supervisors chairman J.J. Bowen a settlement to the problem and wanted a deal. If the jail wall was built on the overlapping strip of his property, he could, at any time and however he chose, use half of the jail wall for any building he might construct. Apparently, Caretto and Bowen came to an amicable settlement, as no more complaints came from the Bisbee man.

The other problem for the new jail was the halting of work due to a delay in getting steel for the cells and plates. The steel was ordered as soon as the contracts were signed but took longer than expected to arrive. It was announced on August 14, 1904, that the steel was finally on its way and was between Chicago and Bisbee on a train. The announcement said that it was expected to arrive within a few days, after which construction would resume.

The jail was finally completed on January 20, 1905 and opened in the early part of February the same year. A newspaper article of January 21, 1905, in the *Bisbee Review*, "Branch Jail Accepted Fund for Inspection," reported that the final contract price for the construction of the jail was

$10,850. The article added that it was the most modern jail in the territory. The jail could now care for thirty-five prisoners. There were six cells on the second floor; the ground floor was to be used to hold those involved in common misdemeanor cases awaiting their day in court. The facility had a guard and a jailer. One stayed on duty during the day; the other took over the nightshift.

The facility stayed open until Bisbee outgrew it. A grander, more modern facility was built around the corner on Naco Road in 1919.

The old building caught the eye of the famous actor John Wayne, and in 1974, he invested a half interest with a business partner named Edwin J. Smart. Smart was the only bidder at a city auction held in January 1973 and bought it for $1,500. Strict terms existed in a lease for the land that the jail was sitting on, as it was controlled by the Phelps Dodge Corporation, which owned it. The terms stated that the buyer had to complete restoration, inside and out, within two years or the building would revert to the city.

Wayne, interested in land and property in Arizona, was already a rancher and landowner in the central part of the state. Smart was good friends with Wayne and brought him to Bisbee to look over the old jail. Wayne was extremely interested in the building and decided he would turn the property into a "John Wayne Museum" that could be developed into a major tourist attraction. He said he would restore the building as a jail with an "old-time" sheriff's office in the front.

The actor's plans were to fill the museum with a sizable collection of his own memorabilia, including various types of guns, costumes used in some of his movies, framed autographed photos and other items. When the museum was completed, Wayne expected to become a rather frequent Bisbee visitor.

Alas, the great film star didn't make the old county jail on OK Street his museum, but it has been refurbished a few times over the decades and still looks great for its age.

The history of this site makes for a unique situation for paranormal activity, due to the two buildings that stood on the same land. Twice as many psychic impressions were left by people who were in dire straits, seeping with emotions of anger and fear.

During many of my historical and haunted tours, several folks told me about their own personal paranormal experiences at the building. For many years, it was called the "OK Street Jailhouse," a short-term rental.

During an afternoon tour, I was outside giving the history of the building to a group when guests staying at the old jail came outside and told us what had happened to them that very morning. One of the two men staying there said he was up before his partner and went downstairs to make coffee. "I felt as if someone was behind me, on my heels, all the way down the steps," the man said. He continued, "But as soon as I stepped onto the ground floor, that heavy feeling stopped!"

The other guest at the time was still lying in bed and said he suddenly felt a heavy hand press against his forehead. Without opening his eyes, he said he playfully swatted at who he thought was his partner. When he did open his eyes, there was no one there.

Another guest on another day staying at the old jail said he heard someone crying and whimpering in the closet on the second floor. The sounds were very faint but loud enough for him to hear.

Many individuals have made comments that while in that building, they have had the feeling of being watched when no one else is in the room, as well as the feeling of haste or anxiety.

I myself had participated in a ghost hunt there and took many photos inside with a film camera. The photographs did not contain much evidence, except those taken on the second floor. I captured over fifty orbs floating from the ceiling to the ground.

These balls of energy most likely belonged to the men who suffered there during their term of punishment. They may have left that heavy and somber emotional pain in the 115-year-old building, which predictably will linger for many years to come.

MIRACLE HILL

OK Street has gorgeous views of the "Gulch" and the houses built on the sides of the mountains across the way, giving one the feeling of an amusement park ride as one drives the old road. At the end of the street is a tiny turnaround and a parking area for OK Street residents. A walking trail beginning at that site leads up the side of Chihuahua Hill.

At the end of the quarter-mile climb is a remarkable site called "Miracle Hill." A sixty-by-fifty-foot religious shrine and Bisbee landmark, it has been visited by thousands since it was created by a retired Bisbee miner named Adolfo Vasquez in 1979.

According to a 1995 article in the *Bisbee News*, Vasquez had poor eyesight and, being a devoted Roman Catholic, said he built the religious monument for God to help him with his sight. He said his sight began to improve as he

Miracle Hill seen from OK Street. The shrine is on top of a mountain marked by a white cross, with remarkable views and where miracles have taken place.

built the shrine on top of the mountain. The land is owned by the Muheim family, who gave him permission to use it.

Vasquez carried bags of cement, bricks, sand and various tools on the approximately thirty-minute walk to the top to build the retreat. He built rock walls and put chairs under shaded areas. Family members brought up plants and cacti to add to the solace of the area. Vasquez also built adobe grottos for statues of the Sacred Heart of Jesus, the Virgin of Guadalupe and the Virgin of Fatima, as well as several patron saints. The Phoenix native also carried the twelve-foot-high, eight-foot-wide white cross to the site, which can be easily seen from below.

It has been reported that many people who have visited the site have had miraculous things happen there. Prayers have been answered and healings and various needs have been met after individuals have stepped onto the religious shrine.

Today, people are still making the hike to Miracle Hill to find consolation and harmony surrounded by beautiful views.

Vasquez passed away in the summer of 2000. According to his obituary, he said that, after his retirement, he had a dream of creating a place where anyone "could find peace and time to be with the Lord."

THE MUHEIM HERITAGE HOUSE MUSEUM

The gorgeous house that stands in the middle of Youngblood Hill Avenue has a remarkable history that evokes the true spirit of Bisbee. The Muheim Heritage House Museum was built by a Bisbee pioneer named Joseph M. Muheim Sr. I have to say, he is my favorite Bisbee forefather and innovator. His palpable presence, ambitious ideas and fantastic business sense made him a Bisbee heavyweight. He spearheaded some enterprising projects.

He answered to two nicknames, "Lucky" and "Joe," and was born in Uri Göschenen, Switzerland, on January 25, 1867. He was a nephew of the Dubacher brothers. He was also referred to as the "grubstake founder of Cananea," a mining town in Mexico. He came to America in 1887 and, the next year, rode into Bisbee by stagecoach from Tombstone. He came to work for his uncles, who were operating a brewery in Brewery Gulch.

He and other associates located several mining claims in Cananea, then sold them to Colonel William Greene for $30,000. Greene ended up making millions of dollars from those mines. Muheim duplicated his business transactions in the Bisbee District. He found mining claims and sold them to big mining companies, which saw the same outcome as Greene.

Muheim, along with his uncles and another prominent Bisbee businessman, Baptiste Caretto, had constructed some of Bisbee's most famous landmarks, including the Pythian Castle on OK Street, the Philadelphia Hotel, the *Bisbee Ore* newspaper building and the "Muheim Block" located in the business district of Brewery Gulch. He was involved in many committees and clubs and was one of the founders of the Miners & Merchants Bank in town. He and his wife, Carmelita, were members of Bisbee's high-society community.

Carmelita LaForge Muheim, from Ironwood, Michigan, was born in 1878. Her parents were French Canadian. Because of Carmelita's accent,

Above: Muheim Heritage House Museum. The walking path alongside the house is where ghostly reports of invisible beings have been seen moving curtains of the side window to peek out.

Right: Joseph M. Muheim Sr., Bisbee pioneer and developer. He was a successful family man who invested in local real estate, mining property and banking.

she had the nickname "Frenchy." She came to Bisbee to live with her sister, who ran a boardinghouse in the area.

Joseph and Carmelita were married in Tombstone in 1898 and moved into the house on Youngblood Hill the same year. Joseph had the home built for his new bride, and it was completed in 1915. The couple had an ever-expanding family, and Joseph had additions made to the house to keep up with the needed space as the years went by. Also, longtime Muheim employee Henry Showers was said to be an extremely slow builder.

The Muheims had four children. Joseph Jr. was born in 1900, Anton was born in 1904, Henry in 1906 and Helen in 1908. Carmelita Muheim was known for her involvement with the building of the YWCA in Bisbee and was an active member of St. Patrick's Roman Catholic Church. She also worked closely with the Loretto Catholic School. She died on February 27, 1947. At the time of his death in 1951, Joseph Sr. was the last surviving original director of the Miners & Merchants Bank.

The Muheim House was a family home until 1973. Henry Muheim lived there until his death that year. In 1975, the remaining children donated the house to the City of Bisbee with a condition that the Bisbee Council on the Arts and Humanities would restore and run it as a living museum. The Muheim Heritage House Museum is an exquisite example of late nineteenth-century architecture and is a wonder to see.

The museum, a National Historic Register site, opened in 1980. The home is on an irregular lot and overlooks a part of the business and residential districts of Bisbee, offering an incredible panoramic view. The house is filled with period furnishings and has been restored to its original elegance. It is located at 207 Youngblood Hill and can be seen from above on OK Street and from Brewery Avenue below.

If you take a tour of the inside of the home, you may instantly feel the strong sense of a male presence as you look to the right of the front door. A round room has an extraordinary window affording a view of Brewery Avenue below. This room may have been the office or working space for Joseph Muheim Sr.

As you walk to the back of the house, where the master bedroom is located, there is a shaving set from the early 1900s set up as an example of daily life. Whether or not this kit is Muheim's, one can sense his alpha-male presence in that room and precisely in that area.

The house has many items that belonged to the Muheim family, including photos of the grown children and grandparents hanging on the wall and set on an upright piano. The energy may be residual, but you can communicate with the spirit of the family that lived there from the time it was built. They give off an elegant, endearing feeling of love and ambition.

The family members were devoted Catholics. The museum has a religious altar on display and a shrine to the Blessed Virgin Mary that is located outside in the large fenced yard.

The house is peaceful and serene, but there have been reports of ghostly activity from locals and Bisbee natives who have witnessed it in the day and at night. The curtains in the side windows of the house nearest to Brewery Avenue moved when the house was empty and not yet a museum. Recent reports have complained of the same events during the museum's after-hours or when it is empty.

There is a set of stairs at the same side that lead to the street. From here, people have used the stairs as a shortcut to get from Brewery Avenue to OK Street without walking up the very steep road, or vice versa. As they walk on a path running right by those windows, they have seen the curtains move as if someone was peeking out. The path is so close to the glass that anyone could see who was looking. But witnesses report that they see no one.

Lights have gone off and on inside as well when people go past the house or when someone is climbing to the top of the set of stairs. The haunting feelings that witnesses have reported were more of a curious nature—who or what is moving the curtains and triggering the lights?—than of fear.

The windows at that side of the house are of the living room and dining room, natural places to peek out to see who is coming up to visit or to watch a friend leave. Either way, the house has a definite immortal feel that seems to revive the period when Bisbee was at its peak of elegance. If Carmelita Muheim described her home as a masterpiece, she may have said it was a pièce de résistance.

4
ZACATECAS CANYON

"LA SPIRITU"

Zacatecas Canyon is an old thoroughfare located at the upper end of Brewery Gulch. It is a secluded neighborhood adjacent to Dubacher Canyon and below Chihuahua Hill. Another way to come in to or travel out of Bisbee is on a gorgeous path currently called Ridge Line Trail.

At the turn of the twentieth century, this part of Bisbee was the neighborhood where Mexicans, Mexican Americans and Yaqui Indians lived. Zacatecas Canyon was a settlement developed around a community dance hall and a saloon or cantina. Here, along with Chihuahua Hill, is where a heavy drape of dramatic and traumatic incidents took place, mostly over one hundred years ago.

In the spring of 1921, an elderly widow living in Zacatecas Canyon was taken away by police for a preliminary examination of her sanity at the local justice court. The *Bisbee Daily Review* reported that Cresencia Andrada de Felix's husband had died nine years before and that she was taken away by authorities due to reports made by neighbors. Even though she was still functioning as if she was content with her life, her neighbors worried, because she became very thin and frail. They told authorities that she never ate and grieved continuously for her husband.

Right before de Felix was taken away for evaluation, her neighbors saw the woman on several occasions walking up the hillside of Zacatecas at night. She would hold a candle in one hand and a large crucifix in the other, seemingly calm and happy. The dim light of the candle cast an eerie glow against the large rocks and bushes. Setting an eccentric and somber scene of a spiritual ritual, the elderly woman was dedicated to her dead husband.

When examined in court, she answered questions concisely and sensibly, then she suddenly and loudly recited some sort of mystical sermon. Dr. H.A. Reese said that she suffered from a mild form of dementia and should be taken care of in an institution. After the doctor testified, the court took his advice and handed the widow her fate.

I could probably fill several chapters with reports of violent and strange incidents that took place in the area of Zacatecas Canyon. I have one of the spookiest and most haunting stories about Bisbee, one filled with mystery, gloom and shocking details.

"Ghostly Visitations Are Disturbing Zacatecas" is the title of the remarkable ghost story printed in the *Bisbee Daily Review* on October 17, 1909. The article states that huge boulders were being thrown down the hillsides by mysterious hands, a woman in white had appeared nightly on the hilltop with long, drawn-out wails, stones were being thrown through windows of houses and strange noises and sights were making life a terror for the settlement known as "Zacatecas."

During the month of October, every night for a week, three officers were called to the canyon to investigate the claims made by several individuals living in the neighborhood. No one had been able to figure out what was happening. The incidents seemed to worsen each time officers were called.

Zacatecas residents said that a "woman in white" made a nightly appearance between 10 p.m. and midnight on the crest of a hill. Reports said she would cry and weep for a few moments, then let out desperate wails. Then she would vanish into the air, followed by a shower of rocks coming from an unknown source.

The paranormal reports began in March 1909. Authorities nicknamed the area "Spook-Land." Horrifically, just before these strange spectacles began, Constable Parley McRae found a two-week-old Caucasian baby wrapped in a blanket on the hillside in the same canyon. He found the baby right above a collection of adobe huts. Bisbee authorities investigated to find the parents of the newborn but were unsuccessful. It is noted that the ghost call-ins to police started the night after the baby was discovered.

The boulders that were rolled down the hillsides were so large that they were able to crash through house doors and damage the sides of two or three structures. Police continuously rushed to the aid of callers to try to catch a glimpse of the person guilty of the destruction, but with each arrival, they saw no one at fault. In fact, it was reported by police that while they stood there trying to figure this puzzle out, they could only stand and listen to the falling stones hitting houses. The perpetrator moved its position so quickly and frantically that the police couldn't see who or what was throwing with such vengeance.

The bizarre rock-throwing suddenly stopped one week after the dead baby was found. But this is when reports shifted to witnesses seeing an "American" (a term Hispanic people use to describe white or Caucasian individuals) woman who would suddenly appear and sit down on the spot where the baby's body was found. People who saw her said she looked unnatural and not of this world.

She would weep and cover her face, her body trembling. This dramatic scene would play out for almost an hour before she would suddenly get up and leave. Witnesses who were brave or foolish enough would chase her. Running hard to keep up, they could barely see her in the night, rushing in front of them and out of reach. They followed her into the wilderness of Dubacher Canyon but could never keep sight of the woman and would lose her every time.

Sightings of the strange woman stopped the following summer, and peace was regained in the canyon. Except, a horrendous incident took place in the hills once more. An unnamed woman was killed near the end of September in Zacatecas Canyon. A drunken woodcutter was carelessly shooting his gun and accidentally hit a few sticks of dynamite with a stray bullet and blew up the hut she was living in.

Following this repulsive death, the paranormal activity started up again. There were reports of a hail of rocks falling on rooftops followed by several huge boulders crashing down the hillside, returning with a higher degree of destruction. A report claimed that one boulder struck the door of a home so hard it smashed it to bits. The invisible perpetrator turned its focus continuously on one house. The occupants of the home were forced to leave. The reports stated that the assaults continued for several hours until dawn.

On top of those bizarre events, another unnerving and creepy situation unfolded in front of the entire neighborhood of Zacatecas. A full-bodied apparition of a woman in white began to appear, then would suddenly vanish. She would stand clearly and boldly on top of the hill for a full minute or two and begin to cry, wail almost uncontrollably, then disappear.

Her long weeping screams echoed across the canyons, sending chills up the spines of everyone who heard her. She was surrounded by just enough radiance to make her figure distinguishable. Her anguish and despair oozed from her terrible moans as if she were howling to express her sadness.

"La Spiritu"—the author's rendition of "The Woman in White," who wailed with despair on a Zacatecas Canyon hilltop, witnessed by hundreds in 1909. *Author's artwork.*

The ghost appeared every night, and the entire neighborhood of Zacatecas was on edge. People were warned not to go there at night, as someone could accidentally be shot. The residents, armed with weapons, were frightened and willing to act on any noise or movement. They began to shoot at the rocks that showered over them and would hear only the thud of their bullets and birdshots hitting the ground.

This eerie, spectral entity that haunted the hilltop, along with the rock- and boulder-throwing, was perplexing to Bisbee authorities, who refused to believe the culprit was a ghost. Constable McRae said that the Zacatecas residents who thought this were out of their minds. He thought that, instead of ghosts causing havoc, it may have been the Yaqui people in the same neighborhood throwing the rocks.

At that time, it was well known that the Mexicans and the Yaquis did not get along. The police figured the Yaquis were harassing the Zacatecas residents and were quick enough to not be seen and to dodge their bullets.

But, as far as the "woman in white" was concerned, authorities said that was an unexplained phenomenon.

None of the officers claimed to see the apparition on the hill, but the Zacatecas residents said she was due to "La Spiritu."

These supernatural events were witnessed by well over one hundred people a century ago, but reports of similar activity have spread to present times. I lived down the road and above Brewery Gulch on Taylor Avenue in my junior high years and, being a Bisbee native and living in the vicinity of Zacatecas, heard many strange stories about that area.

As an older child, I heard the chatter of people that rocks were being thrown at random houses and at people passing by on stairways and trails. People spoke of the sounds of rocks hitting rooftops in the wee hours of the night; when persons checked their homes in the morning to see if they could find any clues, they did. They found the strange tracks of what looked like hooves. But they were in pairs, not in sets of four.

During a book signing I had at Atalanta's Bookstore, which was located on Main Street back in 2004, a woman told me that, years before, as she was walking past Zacatecas and Chihuahua Hill, out of thin air she saw a piece of ember floating down in front of her. Then another came, with a bigger flame of fire. She instinctively looked up and around for a fire but saw absolutely nothing. She could never explain the embers. She said it was a mystical event that she remembered as though it had happened the very day she was talking to me.

Another Bisbee native from the Zacatecas area said that, throughout her life, as she slept in her childhood bedroom, she has heard a woman's scream in the night. She described the sound as coming from above her house and sounding unnatural. Not human. The haunting and wailing cries are loud enough to wake her up but, at the same time, are faint and far away. The witness said she has sat up in her bed in fright many times and closes her eyes and hears the ghostly cries, then they abruptly fade.

Zacatecas Canyon was a stop on my historical and haunted tours. During a few of them, my guests and myself had unexplained experiences in that area. On one night, with a full golf cart of guests, as I finished speaking about the supernatural events that took place there, and in an unusual moment of quiet, pebbles were tossed at us. We were parked close to a hillside, and suddenly, stones were beginning to hit the cart. Random pings hit the side of the vehicle, and little thuds were heard on the roof. We looked at one another, and a member of the tour group asked me if I set this up and said that he didn't think it was funny.

"Hell, no!" I replied.

Then I saw rocks under a streetlight come off the ground, and as if by invisible hands, I saw a stone tossed directly at me. Another tour guest said with a shake in their voice that they were witnessing the same thing. I started the engine of the cart and said, "It's time to go."

Another night, at the same site, I was shushed by a member of my tour group. I immediately stopped talking and heard an echoed sound that at first resembled that of a stray animal, but as the moments passed, the voice became raspy and low. It was near. A woman in the back of the cart let out a scream and pleaded for me to drive away. I kindly obliged.

TEENAGER DROWNS IN McDONALD RESERVOIR

There is an old reservoir at Zacatecas Canyon where residents would go to swim and relax. On August 17, 1921, during monsoon season, some neighborhood children were swimming at McDonald Reservoir, which was full of rainwater. Salvador Bescanio, a sixteen-year-old teenager, and a group of his friends were having a great time in the morning hours that day. Bescanio was sitting on the bank of the reservoir when a little boy came from behind and shoved him into the water. The teenager began to wave his arms about, and he went under a few times before anyone noticed he was in trouble.

A friend jumped in to save Bescanio by grabbing one of his wrists and began to bring him to safety, but the drowning teen grabbed his friend around his neck and began to pull him down along with him. The boy managed to kick himself loose from Bescanio and made it safely to the bank, exhausted. Bescanio instantly sank into the deep water and was never seen alive again.

Some men who were present dove in to look for Bescanio but couldn't find him. Someone called police officers and Judge W.P. Craig to the frantic scene. Another person brought a priest and two divers from Sonora, Mexico, for added prayer and help. The divers were unable to find the teenager in the murky water.

At that point, it was decided to detonate a large number of charges of dynamite in the water in the vicinity of where the teen was last seen, in an attempt to push up the body. This extreme method failed, so hooks and drag nets were used to search for Bescanio, but that also failed. Syphons were used, but that didn't drain sufficient water for the task. James McDonald, the owner of the reservoir, was in Tombstone, and he was called to locate

Floating candles seeking the body of Salvador Bescanio, who drowned in a reservoir, causing an epidemic of fear and panic in Zacatecas Canyon in 1921. *Author's artwork.*

the outlet pipes in order to drain the water. McDonald said that all the pipes were clogged.

While all of this was unfolding, the Mexican priest asked the mother of the missing child to retrieve two pie tins and candles. The holy man put a candle on each pan and sprinkled holy water on them, then he put them down on the water. He lit the candles and pushed them away and began to pray. He told the crowd of worried adults and children that when one of the pans came to rest over the body of Bescanio, its flame would go out.

The moments that turned into minutes were torture for the onlookers. As the sounds of sobs and cries were heard, one of the pans began to float along the edge of the reservoir and into a corner and stopped. The candle's flame went out! People began to shout in Spanish, "Look! Look!"

It was too dark to continue diving that night, regardless of the priest's actions. A crew worked outside of the reservoir to knock down a cement wall to drain the water. Crews expected that the water would be sufficiently drained to recover the body overnight. The reservoir itself was approximately forty-five feet wide and sixty-five feet long, and the water was between ten and twenty-five feet deep. It was said that there was a lot of debris at the bottom; it was suspected that Bescanio's body was caught on some of it.

At 9:00 a.m. the next morning, the body of Bescanio was found in the exact area where the candle had gone out the night before. This was about fifty feet from where the teenager had sunk and died a terrifying death.

In the years since that horrific incident, reports of a woman crying and children screaming have echoed in the area of the old reservoir. This may be residual memories replaying over and over. Many individuals witnessed the youth's drowning, and the fear and anguish and the sounds of crying and yelling were blasted into an eternal place. At the site of the tragedy, the living can be reminded of what took place 101 years ago.

As Brewery Avenue turns into Zacatecas Canyon, some people experience a cold and unsettling change of emotion, from lightness to sullenness. Mind you, it is a gorgeous area that is still wilderness to some extent, and people do live in the neighborhood. But the scenery seems to completely change during the day's dark hours. With all the strange and eerie events that have taken place in Zacatecas Canyon, I do believe that it is one of the most haunted areas in Bisbee.

5

BREWERY AVENUE AND BREWERY GULCH

RED-LIGHT DISTRICT AND BREWERY GULCH HISTORY

Brewery Gulch is located where Main Street turns into Naco Road. At this location, the Dubacher brothers opened a drinkery. They built the Mountain Brewery, which became a popular place and where not only local miners hang out, but travelers also took a rest and had a cold drink. This is where Brewery Gulch derived its name and where the brothers' nephew Joseph Muheim first started to work in Bisbee, as a bartender.

Their saloon was named the "best equipped establishment of its kind in the territory of Arizona." Among the infamous rascals who patronized the brewery were Burt Alvord, Billy Stiles and a woman named "Black Jack."

Brewery Gulch grew along with the rest of the mining community, but it filled its spaces with more lively businesses than those over on Main Street. Brewery Gulch was packed with approximately forty-seven saloons at one time. The number of actual saloons varies in historical documents.

In Upper Brewery Gulch there was another sort of business expanding and gaining momentum. This area was called the "Red-light District." Soon after Bisbee was named, city officials tried to control prostitution without prohibiting it.

In 1892, the Board of Supervisors of Cochise County adopted a law that confined all brothels to a designated area of South Main Street and west of OK Street. Then, in 1897, to place it at a distance from homes of families and respectable wives, mothers and children, the Red-Light District

Brewery Gulch, Bisbee, Arizona. "The liveliest spot between St. Louis and San Francisco."

Remnants of Mable's Cribs, a business of ill repute. These sets of steps are a piece of times gone by in Bisbee's Red-Light District.

was designated to Upper Brewery Gulch and later extended to a part of Zacatecas Canyon.

One of the major factors in Bisbee's incorporation as a city in 1902 was the regulation of vice and brothels. The first act of the new municipality was to ban women from saloons. Despite that, there were over thirty designated spots for hiring women of ill repute in the Red-Light District. There were also opium dens, hop-joints, casinos, cribs and "supposed" boardinghouses. Mexican and Mexican American families lived in the same borough.

The prostitutes endured a crude lifestyle, and it brought brutal consequences, which often put them in dire straits. Among the acts of violence and criminality in this part of town were murders, fights and brawls that sometimes lasted for days; horrific and graphic treatment of young (and sometimes old) women; property damage; theft and even fires.

On the other hand, Bisbee women working in the tenderloin business were given mandatory health tests. The Cochise County Hygiene Board boasted that the Bisbee girls would pass with A-plus grades.

Among the regular visitors to the Red-Light District were U.S. Army soldiers from Camp Naco and the Douglas post nearby. This was great for business, but by 1910, prostitution was completely restricted in Bisbee. With that, prostitutes, their pimps and the owners of whorehouses were said to have packed up and left in groups on the train to El Paso. By April 1, 1910, the era of "Wild Brewery Gulch" was over.

LOUIS MAURE'S GHOST

The area called Upper Brewery Gulch is where Zacatecas Canyon ends and Brewery Avenue begins. As mentioned before, this area during Bisbee's early days was among the places where the majority of residents of Mexican descent lived, along with Chihuahua Hill, Zacatecas Canyon and another part of Bisbee called Tin-Town.

A spooky and surprising article in the *Bisbee Daily Review* about more ghosts in that area, headlined "Haunted House," was published in April 1906.

Next door to a man name Bob McDonald in Upper Brewery Gulch stood a stone house with four bedrooms. There were reports of unearthly groans echoing through the rooms, invisible entities walking through locked doors, sounds of footsteps in the house and unexplained lights. The house had been owned by Louis Maure before he was brutally murdered in the street by a group of men on Christmas Eve in 1904. His death certificate is dated December 25, 1904, and states that he was thirty years of age, was French American and single. The principal cause of death was a fracture at the base of his skull.

Residents of the area believed that the ghost of Maure returned nightly to the scene of his murder. The new owner, Justice Owen Murphy, had possession of the property for several months and had rented the small house to six families, all of whom moved out as soon as they moved in.

Individuals living in the home frantically told their landlord that they clearly heard groans at night and were constantly awakened to the sounds of scuffling and feet dragging on the wood floor. As soon as a light was turned on, the eerie sounds stopped. Each family left the house because they were completely convinced the house was haunted.

Residents of Upper Brewery Gulch believed that the ghost was haunting the stone house because the soul of Maure, who had been savagely beaten in the head with rocks, was unable to rest—his murderers had not been prosecuted for his death.

Like many Bisbee miners, after a long shift underground, Maure was returning from work at 1:00 a.m. As he approached his block, he saw a group of about five men walking in his direction. As he continued to walk forward, and as he got closer, he realized that one of the men was injured and was being carried. Maure didn't realize that the same group had just attempted to rob his neighbor, James McDonald.

One of the robbers had been shot, and the theory is that Maure recognized the men. The gangsters took no chances on him turning them into authorities and attacked him with rocks and boulders. Maure lived for a few hours after the gruesome attack but never regained consciousness to describe or name his killers.

All five men were caught, tried and sentenced to serve time in the Yuma prison for the attempted robbery, but not for Maure's death.

The tiny stone house haunted by Maure's ghost was famous among residents. Because everyone knew about the haunted house, Murphy couldn't get anyone to rent it. It was still believed by the Mexicans and Mexican Americans in Bisbee that Maure's ghost was still roaming the house where he once lived. No one could convince the population otherwise.

THE WILLS HOUSE

On a shapely turn at Upper Brewery Gulch stands a gorgeous set of three Victorian buildings erected by George B. Wills. An English immigrant who registered in the Arizona Territory as a bricklayer in 1898, the thirty-eight-year-old was known for recycling used bricks to construct buildings. He built this complex in an English row house style with recycled material. Wills lived there with his sister and a homeless girl they took in sometime around when the buildings were being constructed.

There are two separate two-story buildings and one single-level structure. The two-story structure farthest to the left was the first one completed, around 1902. It housed three apartments, one being the Wills residence. The building plan seemed not to be thought out carefully at the beginning stages. A stairway between the original structure and the second one covers the window in the ground-floor apartment of the first section of the building. There were eight apartments and one bath in the second building. The single-story building, erected most recently, had five apartments. The apartments were extremely tiny, the smallest being ten feet by ten feet.

This apartment complex stood on the border of Bisbee's Red-Light District. It was rumored that this complex was used as a place for prostitution. Some say the young homeless girl was really a woman of ill repute and the head of the family business.

There was a trapdoor on the front porch of the single-level building. This door led to stairs that went to a passage beneath the porch. Leading off this passage are two rooms, which have doors and windows. These rooms were the same size as two rooms above them. Some say these were used as "cribs" for prostitution purposes and as storage for illegal liquor during Prohibition.

Thomas Constable was another Englishman who became a citizen in the Arizona Territory in 1892. Records show he registered as a forty-three-year-old miner in 1896. He became a longtime tenant in one of the small apartments in the one-story building. A popular gardener for the Copper Queen Hospital, he later had some sort of accident and walked with a bad limp. Constable, a bachelor, raised Greyhound dogs. He had a reputation of chasing neighborhood children and raising his cane to them if they were caught teasing his dogs.

During several of my nighttime Haunted Historical Cart Tours, guests caught, on different occasions, a glowing human figure standing between the two tall buildings. In the photos, it appeared as though the figure was

George Wills's buildings at Upper Brewery Gulch. Of the three structures, one was rumored to be a "crib" and part of the tenderloin business.

peeking around one of the buildings, looking at the tour group. No one claimed to see the apparition with their naked eye, only in the photos.

Footsteps were also heard across the porch of the one-story building. When flashlights were directed at that porch, no one was seen, but the sounds were still heard. Orbs were caught in pictures of the crumbling porch and of the small front yard of the complex.

In recent years, these buildings, currently being used as apartments, were renovated into beautiful living spaces. On a few tours, the owner of the complex invited my guests and myself inside for a quick tour of one of his buildings. The owner explained how the shotgun-style apartments were laid out and what materials he used to carefully renovate the spaces. He allowed my small tour to do a quick ghost hunt of the apartment we were in.

We went outside. In the small yard in the back, one of my guests began to communicate with a male entity. She asked the spirit's name and received only a murmured voice saying that he was proud of his place.

She asked if he was pleased with the new renovations, and the answer was "yes." To confirm their conversation, she asked for the spirit to make a noise. We had waited only a few moments when a rock hit the top of the roof. Since we were standing in the outside space of the first building on the second floor, the roof was slightly above our heads. The noise startled us. It made us jump a little.

Was the tour guest communicating with Mr. Wills? Was the glowing entity seen between the two buildings the spirits of the gardener of the old Copper Queen Hospital, still standing guard of his beloved Greyhounds? Did the phantom footsteps at the single-story building and the orbs photographed in the complex's community front yard belong to prostitutes or to a few of their clients?

Regardless, the paranormal activity surrounding those buildings is intriguing. The red-brick structures look hauntingly serene as they stand quietly and with much sophistication in a quiet part of the neighborhood of Upper Brewery Gulch.

BISBEE'S CITY PARK

Bisbee's first city cemetery, located between Opera Drive and Brewery Avenue, was created sometime in the late 1880s. After it had deteriorated to ruins, it was closed as a cemetery and transformed into a city park. Another theory as to why the cemetery closed is that it was a public-health concern.

As the burial ground was upslope from water wells, the water would be contaminated, causing or adding to the typhoid outbreaks taking place in the town's early history.

A collage of photos in the *Bisbee Daily Review* of February 2, 1913, shows laundry being dried on some of the fences surrounding the graves of the dead. Tombstones were falling apart and in shambles. The old cemetery had become an eyesore. Maybe the grave sites were in that condition because there wasn't family left in Bisbee to tend to them. The majority of those buried there were single men and people from other countries without family nearby. The site was also an embarrassment and a danger to neighborhood children.

As early as 1910, complaints were being brought to the city council as residents sought a solution. That same year, a petition was presented by I.W. Wallace on behalf of the board of education to the city council to use the site of the old cemetery for a school building to segregate children of African descent. Plans were eventually brought to the council, but the board and Bisbee residents chose to use the property for a playground instead. Children were already using the old cemetery as a play area anyway. If they weren't there, they were running in the narrow streets, barely avoiding cars, horses and wagons—a chaotic and unsafe situation.

According to an announcement made in the *Bisbee Daily Review* in March 1913, a playground committee was formed by the Warren District Commercial Club to plan for a park for the neighborhood children. Another *Bisbee Daily Review* article, "Dilapidated Graveyard or Playground, Which?," reported that members of the committee, during a council meeting, explained the law regarding city and town cemeteries enacted by the legislative assembly of the territory of Arizona. The law reads that whenever any ground used as a cemetery within any city limits has been abandoned and ceases to be used for such purposes or is unfit or unsuited or becomes obnoxious, and if it can be used for other public purposes to better advantage, the city or town can use the grounds and it is to be vacated. The remains of the persons buried there can be removed to another cemetery or suitable place. The expense of such removal is to be paid by the city or town.

The law also reads that, when remains are removed, all monuments and gravestones shall also be removed and placed at the new cemetery. The graves are to be numbered and a list of the names of the buried kept. The notion of abandoning the old cemetery was made fairly easily. During a special meeting with the city council in January 1913, Secretary J.H. Gray of the commercial club said, "We want to place all of these bodies where they will be decently cared for, where the graves will be kept as they should be. We want no desecration of graves but on the contrary, want them made sacred."

Money was raised to renovate the neglected monstrosity, to move the bodies buried in the pioneer burial ground to a new site in Lowell called Evergreen Cemetery and to buy playground equipment.

On April 25, 1913, one of the most despicable events took place at the old cemetery. The *Bisbee Daily Review* ran this incredible headline on April 26: "Brought Head from Battle—Gruesome Souvenir of Naco Engagement Found in the Street Yesterday—Interred by Authorities." The article reported that Chief of Police Bassett Watkins received a frantic call to rush to the old cemetery up Brewery Gulch. He dropped everything he was doing. As soon as he arrived, he noticed a crowd of people standing in a circle. He was told nothing about what he was about to see.

He pushed his way through and, shockingly, saw a human head lying on the ground! The head, already in a bad stage of decomposition, was a revolting sight.

After some investigating, it was discovered that individuals had brought the head from Naco. Their intention was to leave it in a saloon nearby as a kind of souvenir for all to admire. The owner of the saloon refused to have it on the premises and had it taken to the cemetery. It was placed in a shallow grave and, unfortunately, was dug up by a dog.

That same day, the chief had the disembodied head placed in a deeper hole in the cemetery. This time, a pile of rocks was placed over it so that it wouldn't be disturbed again.

The removal of bodies to Evergreen Cemetery began around January 19, 1915, and was completed on January 22. The Palace and Undertaking Company had the contract to clear the cemetery. There were badly organized records of the dead written only in pencil on various pieces of paper. A large number of the plots were labeled "unknown," including an "unknown" baby. John Tappiner was listed as twenty-five years old when he was killed during the Bisbee Massacre and was listed in grave 3. S.8 E.G.

Another notable person buried there was George Warren. An article from 1905 in the *Bisbee Daily Review* stated that George Warren had died in his lonely cabin and his body was buried in the cemetery in the vicinity of the Bisbee Opera House. In the same paper in March 1914, an article with the headline "Monument to Mark Newly Found Grave of George Warren" stated that in an inconspicuous part of the old cemetery, members of the Bisbee Elks Club found his gravesite. They found a worm-eaten and weather-beaten, wood headboard with very faint carved letters, "G.W." The

Elks Club organization investigated and learned that this grave did indeed belong to the infamous George Warren.

Some were nervous that not all the bodies were removed, but there was a diplomatic and vigilant transfer of the graves to Evergreen Cemetery before construction and landscaping of the park began. Of the thirty-four bodies removed and relocated, twenty-three were identified. The last recorded person to be buried there was in 1898, the infant son of H.M. Woods.

The City Park had a formal dedication on May 20, 1916, with Governor George W.P. Hunt in attendance. Memorial Day, the Fourth of July, important political meetings and other events were held here. The city also used the public park for ceremonies for draftees leaving for war and for dances. The park was perfect for such events, as it has a grand bandshell and a smooth concrete floor. However, one person was quoted as saying that she would never attend a dance at City Park, for she was not sure that all the bodies had been removed, and she refused to dance on the dead.

When I was a junior high student, my family moved into the Brewery Gulch neighborhood and lived in a house directly above City Park. At the

Today's Bisbee City Park. It was once a cemetery where thirty-four bodies were removed and relocated to Evergreen Cemetery. Twenty-three of the bodies were identified.

The site where paranormal activity of a ghost-boy has been captured. EVPs, photos of white shadows and object-controlled evidence were collected here in recent decades.

entrance off of the seventy-five steps on the street-free side of the park, I met up with a ghost, a boy. In my book *Mi Reina: Don't Be Afraid*, I wrote of the experience.

I often entered the park through that entrance, and that is where we would often bump heads. He wasn't evil, and he didn't give me a feeling of danger—rather an emotion of despair. I saw an apparition of the boy-ghost next to a permanently stationed green trash can several times. I saw flashes of a young male pointing, showing me his mother's grave. We know that there are no body-filled coffins under City Park, but I do remember feeling that he was a very domineering person. I also felt that he was protecting or watching over something nearby or at the entrance. I saw him pointing at the ground and telling me that this is hallowed ground and not a place for children to play.

Meanwhile, in 2004, Debe Branning, director of MVD Ghostchasers out of Mesa, held a ghost workshop in town and visited the park. We were friends and shared our ghost enthusiasms. We had met in 2000, when I was a reporter for a local newspaper and covered her group's all-day ghost hunt of haunted hotels in Bisbee.

Debe realized after she read my book that she had had a paranormal experience at the same area. She said that, while speaking at the same entrance, she suddenly felt a spine-tingling cold breeze rush thorough her. She then felt nauseous and dizzy. Days later, whenever she looked in a mirror, a young boy would somehow shadow her own reflection. Later, when she read about my experience at the same site, we, along with Sheila Bontreger, another member of the MVD Ghostchasers, got together and went back.

We stood at the park entrance. Debe asked me to stand where I sensed the boy. I did. She said that was the same spot where she had her experience. She grabbed a long twig and put it on the ground. We asked the boy a series of questions and asked that he respond by moving the twig. She videotaped the séance.

He was asked if he remembered me. His response was "yes." We asked his age. We listed the numbers from nine to fourteen. The twig moved at twelve. We asked if his mother had been buried here. He answered "yes." We asked if she was still buried there. He answered "yes." We asked if he was protecting her. He answered "yes." We asked if he wanted to leave. He said "no."

After a while, he stopped responding. He seemed to vanish or simply grew too tired to communicate. The spirit most likely does not realize that his mother's body was removed, and he still haunts the site where her grave used to be.

City Park was another stop on my haunted tour, and I had many more paranormal experiences there. Once during a tour as I was speaking, the large bow on my jacket was untied in front of my guests by invisible hands! On several occasions, I have seen a figure in my peripheral view when no one was standing there. As soon as I am on that site, the ghost rushes to my side. Since Branning had the experience of the boy-ghost following her home, I insist that he does not have permission to follow me. I also encourage guests of my tours to tell him out loud or to themselves not to follow them.

Other tour guests have recorded a male voice at the same spot and have taken pictures of a white fog in sunny daylight. The entrance is not the only place where paranormal activity has been reported. A guest refused to walk near a tree by the street gate, as she saw a tall person standing still, watching and listening to the tour. She said it was an unnatural being and couldn't decipher if it was a ghost or a demon. This frightened her so much that we had to cut the tour short and leave.

City Park is a great place still being used for entertainment, fundraisers, relaxation and as a playground. Exactly what the commercial club intended.

HERMITAGE SALOON

The Hermitage Saloon was a popular hot spot in Brewery Gulch. It opened on May 6, 1904. Today, the only thing left of the tavern is a tile sign in a sidewalk marking the site. It was owned and operated by Sid Harris and George Roberts. In 1905, Roberts bought out Harris and became the sole owner.

Roberts and Harris moved their business into what was previously known as the St. Louis Beer Hall. The space was upgraded with the latest bar fixtures, including a regular soda fountain. The new business bragged that it had the latest Babcock icebox, which could hold imported cheeses and canned meat with which to serve German lunches.

The two-story building had a summer beer garden upstairs, arranged with antique oak tables and metal chairs. Palms and flowers decorated the beer hall. The floors both upstairs and downstairs were covered with linoleum, and a brand-new walkway was in front of the building. The entire interior of the Hermitage was painted snow white.

In 1906, boxing matches—and gambling—were offered at the establishment with $1,000 purses. The matches were so successful that, by 1920, the manager of the Bisbee Athletic Club had bought the saloon to

All that is left of the grand Hermitage Saloon after a fire engulfed the building, an event that was predicted by a psychic sixty-seven years before.

open a gymnasium on the second floor. At that time, the saloon was a soft-drink emporium, as wet days were outlawed during Prohibition. The soft-drink business stayed open while the training quarters were running. The gymnasium had a complete set of workout equipment as well as showers and dressing rooms.

Many sorts of people traveled through the Hermitage during its existence. In 1909, a fortune-teller made a prophecy that a fire would destroy the saloon and Brewery Gulch sometime later that year. The psychic may have gotten the year wrong, but a few fires did occur. On March 3, 1911, at 10:00 p.m., a small explosion across the street from the Hermitage took place. A giant tamale pot being heated with gasoline had exploded. The flames reached across the road and set a shoeshine stand outside the saloon on fire. Just as the flames were reaching the cash drawer of the shoe stand, Reserve Fire Chief French saw the fire and ran through the Hermitage doors with a seltzer bottle and set a steady stream on the flames. The fire was out, but a flame had traveled its way into the cash drawer and set fire to a shoe brush. The fireman put more seltzer water on it while a man named Leo Cannon helped with more water. No significant damage was done to any of the businesses during that mishap.

But on November 9, 1913, a large fire broke out just after 5:25 p.m. from a roof of the Tovres & Co. meat market building located between the Hermitage and the Medigovich building. For fifteen minutes, firemen fought the blaze with hundreds watching. Brewery Gulch was evacuated, and as bystanders left the scene, they only offered help if it was needed.

Two visitors from New York were passing by in the street and were the ones who initially noticed the fire. After setting off the fire alarm, they broke into the meat market to see if anyone was inside. The men's clothes were scorched, but they were unharmed.

The cause of the fire was defective wiring. A small fire in the roof of the building burned slowly, then it broke into a large fire from the entire middle of the wood roof of the building with flames several feet high. Firefighters surrounded the building the best they could and at the same time protected the Hermitage, Medigovich and Shattuck buildings.

The blaze was put out; embers smoldered until 9:00 p.m. Apparently, some of these embers caused a small fire against the side of the Hermitage shortly after the firemen left. A manager of Boston & Brown discovered the outbreak and sprayed seltzer water on it.

Decades later, it seemed that the fortune-teller's prediction finally came true. The Hermitage building was used by the *Brewery Gulch Gazette*, a Bisbee newspaper, along with a companion publication called *Pay Dirt*. On May 12, 1976, a fire destroyed everything and caused $250,000 in damage. The building was destroyed by arson. The blaze not only destroyed the printing press, but it also scorched historic photos, supplies and stock of paper. The old Hermitage Saloon building was turned to ashes. A terrifying prophecy was finally realized sixty-seven years later.

May Gillis's House of Ill Repute at Broadway Avenue

There is a remarkable stairway leading up from Brewery Avenue to an alley at the rear of the Central School building that is named Broadway Avenue. When it was constructed, it looked more like a boardwalk. Sometime in its existence, concrete steps replaced the wood planks. Regardless of that, it pretty much looks as it did over one hundred years ago.

In my paranormal journal from 2004, *Mi Reina: Don't Be Afraid*, I wrote about this site and my unique experience there. Here's an excerpt.

As a young girl in the late seventies, Brewery Gulch was a lot more suitable for families to live in. Saloons were still there, but now called bars and gambling and a Red-light District was no longer legal.

By the end of the school day, I would forget the uneasy time of night by enjoying the sunlight of the afternoon during the bus ride home after a full day of sixth grade.

I would step off the school bus at the Lyric Theater stop and begin my walk home through several shortcuts. Instead of walking through the Gulch to get home (I was not allowed to walk past St. Elmo's bar situated in the middle of the street. I had to literally walk around the neighborhood.) I would walk through the Copper Queen Hotel's plaza, back to the pool and out the back gate. Beyond the hotel's fence is an alley leading up to a set of stairs that finished with the road to my house. In between the hotel and the staircase are another set of stairs, called "Broadway steps" that lead down into Brewery Gulch.

After arriving home from a late Saturday matinee at the Lyric, I interrupted a private conversation between my mother and her friend. My mother asked me to go outside and said she needed the privacy.

I decided to take a walk. As I left my front porch, I noticed the desert sky turning to the glow of orange, purple and sorbet pink. These were the colors of low but energizing cosmic energy.

Broadway steps. This haunted stairway leads past an old house that was used as a brothel a century ago.

I headed toward the place where I found complacency. That sweet place was the Broadway stairway. The stairs are ancient and produce an incredible amount of vitality from its exciting past, plagued with energies from those who have traveled its path.

As I made my journey toward my spot, I began to take in the sweet smells of the Trumpet Honeysuckle vines growing on most of the chain-linked fences of small houses that lined Taylor Avenue. To get to my destination, I had to take another set of cement steps that were steep and to the left side of Central School.

As I descended the stairs, my stomach tightened, and my fingers began to tingle. As soon as I caught the first glimpse of my favorite spot, I began to jog toward it. When I got to the top of the staircase, I stood on the first step for a few seconds before stepping down more. The sun was still shining down through the thick branches of trees and pomegranate bushes lining the sides of the stairway, causing the cement to glimmer and shine.

As I strolled down the stairs, I began to smile. I happily tugged at the leaves brushing my head and found a spot to sit down. I closed my eyes and began to meditate.

Almost immediately, I felt a breeze around me. The dead leaves scattered on the surrounding ground began to slide and hop toward each other, making scratching sounds on the concrete. The dry material gained momentum in the gentle wind. As the breeze took strength, I opened my eyes to the small cyclone of leaves twirling in midair.

Just then, the essence of a light perfume became evident and intensified as each motion of the spiral of dead leaves took speed.

I wasn't frightened at first, but my senses were filled with the energy of several presences. They were of young women whose voices began to whisper. I couldn't understand their words but could hear all of the different tones of voices. I asked them who was there and what did they want.

The sound of soft whispers grew to an ear cracking volume accompanied with numerous pairs of feet shuffling around the stairs, positioning themselves completely around me. The entities executed depressed emotions, bringing me to tears. That is when I closed my eyes and vivid pictures of each entity were etched into my thoughts and soul.

I saw a small and fair-skinned Mexican woman, wearing an off white, underwear looking, linen material with a tight bodice covering her tiny waist. She was whispering, "…help me."

There was also a chubby blonde who appeared to be middle aged and wrinkled. Lastly there was the third, she was beautiful. Her long, dark and wavy hair was pulled back with oversized, silver hair combs.

In a sudden and astonishing moment, a feeling of holy terror rang through my bones. Screeches of blood curdling screams forced me to cover my ears as jolts of a pain shot through them.

The echo of shrieks from the female apparitions, suppressed extreme anxiety, slinging the spirits together into one large white cluster of fog, that zipped quickly up to the top of the stairs, with the poignant screams following closely behind. The ball of mist sifted to the left of the stairway and disappeared, leaving a haunting silence in its place.

As an adult, I realize that my encounter on that thoroughfare was with the ghosts of women who were part of the infamous tenderloin business in Bisbee over one hundred years ago. I have also discovered that there was a woman named May Brown with the alias "May Gillis" who was arrested for running a brothel on the same site where I had that haunting experience.

An article in the *Bisbee Daily Review* of April 23, 1912, "Raid House That Is Near a School—Immoral Place Can't Be Run within 400 Yards of Public School," reported that a residence on Broadway had been raided by City Marshal Bassett Watkins and Night Officer Walter Brooks on April 21.

The residence had been under investigation for some time, and when it was raided in the early part of the day, two individuals were arrested for keeping and residing in houses for "immoral" purposes located within four hundred yards of a school. Unfortunately for them, the school was less than fifty yards from the Central School.

May Gillis pleaded guilty and was sentenced to pay a fine of fifty dollars. She ended up at the county branch jail for fifty days because she couldn't pay the fine. The other person arrested was Victor Sitner. He pleaded not guilty and demanded a trial, which was set for April 26. He was released on bond for twenty-five dollars.

Gillis had a rowdy reputation and a depressing past. In 1905, she was staying at the Elite Lodging House over on Main Street and mistakenly drank carbolic acid. The newspaper reported that she had claimed she had a very bad headache in the middle of the night and made the mistake of drinking the entire bottle of the acid, mistaking it for medicine she had in her room. Some say she tried to kill herself but that, because of the pain in her mouth and throat from the fiery acid, her screams of anguish saved her life. She ended up in jail a few times after that, including for trying to shoot Sitner. Sadly, she was committed to the asylum by the Lunacy Commission, composed of D.H.H. Hughart and C.R. Baker, in 1916.

This kind of anomalous commotion, along with robberies, gambling, drinking and the dance halls, saloons, restaurants and hotels on either side of the narrow gulch, is why the area was given the winning title "The Liveliest Spot between St. Louis and San Francisco."

6

HOTELS AND INNS

SCHOOL HOUSE INN BED & BREAKFAST

There is a very special building near the top of Tombstone Canyon. It was built in 1918, and for two decades it housed vibrant, enthusiastic first-through fourth-graders. Garfield School was constructed as Bisbee was rapidly growing—a school was being built every half mile. The two-story brick building gallantly sits above its own terraced playground, which now belongs to the city and is named after the old school: Garfield Park. As for the school, it is now a nine-room bed-and-breakfast called the School House Inn, owned and run by John Lambert and Paula Roth.

Garfield School closed in 1938 and was turned into an apartment building. The classrooms were very big and were easily converted into desirable living spaces by adding walls. The twelve-foot ceilings are remarkable and most likely were designed to keep the classrooms warm during those cold, mile-high winter days in the Tombstone Canyon mountains. Bathrooms with showers were added for apartment living.

According to John R. Kibbey Architects' 1917 blueprints of the original building, the basement held the furnace room and the fuel room for storing coal. The original steam-heated furnace is still there. The first floor of the school is where the four classrooms were located. The rooms had maple floors, picture molding and wainscot railing. Each classroom was about thirty-two feet by twenty-four feet, with additional space for cloakrooms or closets.

School House Inn. This converted elementary school built in 1918 was turned into a gorgeous inn at the top of Tombstone Canyon.

The boys' bathrooms were on the west side of the school; on the other end of the building were the girls' bathrooms. There was an office and library, as well.

Some decades later, the building was also used as a home for the elderly and was finally turned into a bed-and-breakfast in the late 1980s called the Petra Bed & Breakfast. In the 1990s, Mark and Shirl Negus bought it and renamed it the School House Inn Bed & Breakfast and ran it for about five years.

Lambert said he had heard about Bisbee and decided to take Roth on a special trip to the southeastern Arizona town. The couple were in the dining area when they heard from the owner at the time that he was selling the inn. The couple was enjoying their stay so much that they decided, on the spot, to buy it.

The spacious rooms are named the Art Room, Music Room, Geography Room, History Room, Writing Room, Reading Room, Arithmetic Suite, Principal's Office Suite and Library Suite.

This 102-year-old building has had numerous reports of paranormal activity and is currently accumulating more.

There are antique toys set in the hallways of the inn to go with the school theme, and every now and then, a doll carriage moves on its own. Roth said she passes the carriage several times a day, especially when she is making up rooms for the arrival of new guests. She recalled one of those times.

The carriage she is speaking of sits against the wall and has several vintage dolls inside. She remembers walking with many sets of sheets to a room and had forgotten an item, so she instantly walked back out into the hall. As she was hurrying along, she almost fell over the buggy. She said that she was surprised when she saw the object in the middle of the hallway. This is a conundrum, as the floor is level and there is nothing to push the doll buggy forward. The owners said this event usually takes place around January and February.

A guest staying in the Geography Room went downstairs at 2:00 a.m. to get some tea. As he was coming up the stairs to return to his room, he could hear kids laughing and giggling. The chilling sounds of giggling children in

This antique baby-doll carriage has mysteriously moved on its own in an area near the inn's personal residence, the Teacher's Lounge.

Left: A hallway where the eerie sounds of ghostly children laughing have been heard by School House Inn guests.

Right: The Arithmetic Room is the site of reports of an apparition of a woman dressed in nineteenth-century clothes. She levitates, circles the room, then disappears through a wall.

an empty hallway, in the middle of the night, was described by the guest as extremely creepy.

In the Arithmetic Suite, a full-bodied apparition of a woman wearing an 1880s long, flowing gown was seen. A guest told the owners of the inn that when she was trying to get to sleep, she was amazed to see, in a corner of a room, the astonishing sight. She said the woman was levitating and moved around the room and seemed to be looking around, as if she was sizing things up. Then, after a few moments, she disappeared through the wall!

A man staying in the History Room said that while he was sleeping, someone tugged and pushed his leg to the side and woke him up. No one was around him. When he went to lie back down, he felt someone pulling on his leg again. The guest described the scene as very scary.

Another visitor said the music box in the History Room started playing out of nowhere, when no one was near it. In the same room, a door opened slowly on its own.

One evening, Lambert said he was sitting in his apartment, located at an end of the long hallway, when he saw a shadow go past the door. He said to himself, "Oh, somebody is in the building." He was surprised, since it was a quiet night and no one was booked. So, he got up and opened the door and poked his head out, looked down the hall and didn't see anyone. He sat back down and saw the shadow go back and forth a few more times. The window in the door is obscured glass, so he couldn't clearly see who it might have been—only the haze of a bodily figure passed by.

In the Writing Room, Roth said that, on different occasions, after she has made up the bed and then come back into the room, there has been an impression of a body in the bed.

During one of my tours at the inn, as guests were taking pictures up and down the hallways, I began to take pictures myself. As I stood at the end of the hallway, a guest was on the other side. As he walked toward me, I could see, in my camera phone, a thick, white ball walking with him. As I took the picture, the ball moved with him and was in every frame.

INN AT CASTLE ROCK

At the point where Tombstone Canyon Road turns into Bisbee's Main Street sits the Inn at Castle Rock. Originally the Murihead House, a boardinghouse for miners, it was built over the Apache Spring in 1895.

Joseph J. Murihead, the owner and Bisbee's first elected mayor, had come to Bisbee around 1880 and was a miner for the Copper Queen Mining Company. The building, in the Queen Anne style with wraparound verandas, was the largest structure in Bisbee at the time.

The Apache Spring Well was created after a mining shaft was built there in the late 1880s and is still running. It's a sight to see inside the Inn at Castle Rock.

Murihead was born in Ontario, Canada, in 1849 and died in Bisbee on March 1, 1930. His life was remarkable. Besides being the mayor, he also was part of the organization of Bisbee's first Lodge of Free and Accepted Masons and was a Knight Templar, a Shriner, a member of the Eastern Star and a founder of the Episcopal church in Bisbee.

His wife, Catherine Jane Murihead, was the first president of the Bisbee Women's Club, the first organized women's club in Arizona. Catherine ran the boardinghouse until 1948. In later years, the building became apartments. By the 1980s, it had been turned into a hotel and, after 2009, was restored to its original appeal and charm. The hotel, with fourteen themed rooms, is now owned by Chris Brown.

Above: The Inn at Castle Rock, originally the Murihead House and home of Bisbee's original water well, which is still running and is located inside the establishment.

Right: The site where Mabel Watters was shot and killed in 1935. She is said to now haunt the Inn at Castle Rock, looking for her killer.

On October 13, 1935, a thirty-four-year-old woman named Mabel Watters, a mother of two children and wife of a Bisbee miner, was walking up the street and passing Castle Rock by herself in the late afternoon. At that very moment and across the street, a twenty-three-year-old man named Norman Duke, a mining motor man for the Copper Queen Mining Company, was cleaning his hunting rifle in front of a window facing Castle Rock. His gun accidentally discharged from the rooming house. A bullet hit Watters in the neck, killing her instantly. Her death certificate stated the cause of death as a gunshot wound at the base of the brain. Duke said he was cleaning the gun for a deer hunting trip and did not realize it was loaded. After a short investigation of the shooting, the death was declared an accident and no charges were brought against Duke.

After such a traumatizing event on that sidewalk across from the hotel, it's not surprising that the ghost of Watters haunts the site. People have reported seeing an apparition of a slender woman in black walking past and very near to them on the sidewalk across from the Inn at Castle Rock, then suddenly fading or just disappearing.

Guests in the hotel have seen the apparition of a woman going from room to room, as if she is looking for something or someone. It is thought that Watters is looking for the person who shot and killed her on that fall day and won't rest until she knows who ended her young life so abruptly.

BISBEE GRAND HOTEL

The original Bisbee Grand Hotel was built in 1906. Two years later, on October 14, 1908, a fire started there that ended up being the most epic fire in Bisbee's history. The fire spread through most of the business district on Main Street. According to a *Bisbee Daily Review* article published the following day, if a water hose had been available, the fire would've been extinguished within a few minutes.

According to the newspaper, the fire started at 6:10 p.m. in the Grand Hotel, located on the corner of Subway and Main Streets, and raged for three hours. The blaze started in a closet of the hotel and was first seen by Sam Frankenberg from the Fair store and a man named Tommy Blair. The men told the newspaper that if they had a house hose, they could have easily put the small fire out. They would've been able to stop a fire that destroyed the hotel before traveling down Main Street and then up to Clawson Hill, leaving only two houses standing. It was reported that

The Grand Hotel, best described as magnificent and richly historical. *Photo courtesy Jenny Chavez.*

the heat of the fire was so fierce that it turned water into steam before it could reach the fire!

After the fire devoured the Grand Hotel, it headed down the road and hurled across Subway Street and caught the Fair building on fire, then spread to the Johnson-Henninger building, better known as the Woolworth building. This structure became a firewall, stopping the blaze from traveling farther down Main Street. The flames were so high and wide that the Anguis Block building across the street was set on fire. Luckily, a side wall of that structure blocked the brutal flames from feeding off any other buildings farther east.

Acting like a live creature, it turned itself around to spread toward upper Main Street and to a part of the residential district on Clawson Hill. Since this was a mining community and dynamite was fairly easily available, it was used to blow up some buildings near Castle Rock to create a firebreak. It worked, but the fire caused $750,000 worth of damage.

Fortunately, no one was killed during the impressive fire, but there were some very terrifying escapes. A four-year-old boy named Weldon was on the third story of the hotel, sick with typhoid fever. He was rescued by an unknown man and carried out of the building, narrowly escaping a burning death. Another escapee from the fire, a plumber named Toney Estes, jumped from the third floor into a blanket.

J.H. Jack, from Los Angeles and the owner of the hotel, came into Bisbee on October 20 to look over the ruins. He said he wasn't sure he was in a position to decide if he would rebuild. But that same day, he stated that it was his intention to build another structure on his lots as soon as the insurance had been adjusted and the necessary arrangements were made.

As of February 27, 1909, it was reported in the local newspaper that the former site of the three-story Grand Hotel was an unsafe and unsightly wood structure. But it was being replaced by a brick and mortar building.

In a photograph called "Main Street, Bisbee. Morning After," a view from the east end of Main Street looking west, visible in the foreground are the buildings that were not burned or destroyed. Visible in the background is the skeleton of the Grand Hotel and the complete devastation of a smoldering blank canvas, as well as a perfect view of Castle Rock.

By the middle of the 1980s, the Grand was restored to its gorgeous Edwardian charm. The rooms were decorated with various themes. Today, the hotel is still basking in the same ornate style. On the second floor, a gorgeous banister surrounds the opening of the floor from the staircase and a large skylight makes it very bright with the Arizona sunshine. On the first floor is the Saloon, with an exquisite wood bar from the same era.

I wrote about a ghost hunt with the MVD Ghostchasers from Mesa in my 2004 book. An excerpt follows:

> The manager of the Grand Hotel of the time gave full permission for our group to look around. As members of the group wandered in and out of empty rooms, I chose to enter Room 2. Here, I felt the presence of a man, but had a stronger sense of some twenties to thirties-aged woman. I said a "lady" not a prostitute. Something "she" made sure I understood.
>
> In another room, a set of child spirits was imprinted, around the ages of five and six. Their giggles were heard, as they happily played alone and unattended by a mother or father.
>
> In the same second floor lobby, the energy of a long-time attendant was felt. The entity travels from the staircase, around the banister and heads toward the outside balcony. A constant piece of memory tape repeated over and over.
>
> Back in Room 2, an orb was photographed, but no others were recorded elsewhere. This hotel didn't feel heavily inhabited with negative supernatural flow, making this place a harmonious medium.

I was part of a dance group at the same time the hotel was restored in the mid-1980s. My group was asked to perform a cancan routine for the Grand's re-opening. We were told by the owners that, during the restoration, a construction worker was on the second floor and, for an instant, saw a woman running from room to room at the end of the hall. He went to look for her but came to realize that he was the only person in the hotel at the time.

Guests have reported seeing an apparition of a female spirit in a Victorian-period dress and hairstyle on the second floor. People have seen this ghost standing at the foot of their bed in the Victorian Room in the middle of the night. She is usually seen in Room 2 or 3.

In the hotel's saloon, there have been countless reports regarding a male apparition who shows himself in the mirror of the women's bathroom. Bartenders over the years have reported that a male presence is strong in the storage room and have had experiences of being touched in that space and also in the saloon itself.

During another ghost hunt at the Grand, Debe Branning and Sheila Bontreger, two members of the Ghostchasers, as well as myself—now a member—had more contact with the female spirit. The investigation was a short one, but the hotel was empty at the time, so we had the place to ourselves.

Branning stepped into a room in the northwest hallway and said she saw a mist forming near the door to the bathroom. She said it was getting very cold in there.

Bontreger and I entered the room as the misty shape dissipated. A few seconds after that, we all walked into the hall and saw that a light was on in the room across from us. It was decided that the ghost wanted us to follow her into that room.

We were standing there until Bontreger decided to go over to the room's bathroom and investigate on her own. All of a sudden, she said, "Someone just touched my arm! I felt a cold breeze and she bumped my arm on the way out!"

That left us with a confirmation of the female ghost at the Grand. After that encounter, we ended the investigation, satisfied and joyous with the experience.

Bisbee Tourism Center (BTC)

As you enter "Old Bisbee" on Naco Road, you will see almost immediately a grand, two-story building with four massive pillars and ornate trim. The impressive style dates it to the year 1918, when it was constructed. This official-looking building opened in early 1919. The $10,000 structure was

Bisbee Tourism Center, a place for tours, shuttles, Bisbee merchandise, food and accommodations. Did I mention the ghosts lurking inside? *Photo courtesy Bisbee Tourism Center.*

used by the city and county. It is now the Bisbee Tourism Center (BTC), a hotel, restaurant and touring business.

The city marshal and deputy sheriff offices, the justice of the peace office and a courtroom and jury room were upstairs. I.C.E. Adams, the Cochise County Board of Supervisors chairman, established an office for himself on the second floor. The jail cells were located downstairs and held thirty prisoners, with a jailor on duty twenty-four hours a day. Many of the original cell bars and doorways are still in existence. In fact, the former holding cell and solitary confinement area are intact and can be viewed as part of the tourist attraction of the building.

Chief Marshal J.A. Kempton kept a tight ship at the building and was well known around town. He was abrupt and strict. He was also in charge of animal control and, the same year the building opened, commissioned M. Jaso as the official burro catcher of Bisbee. Donkeys were as common as pet dogs with some families in the mining town; at one point, the donkey population was too high. This is when Marsal Kempton thought of hiring a donkey catcher as a way to bring those numbers down. On Jaso's first day, he rounded up six donkeys by noon.

Vagrancy was also on Marshal Kempton's mind. He brought many men in to see Judge John W. Hogan for being idle, in violation of the city ordinance against vagrancy. Judge Hogan gave out stiff sentences, including sixty days on the road gang and time in jail.

As news of the vagrancy roundup went around town, the men who would at all times of the day happily sun themselves in front of the fence of the Phelps Dodge general office (today, the Bisbee Mining & Historical Museum) seemed to disappear.

Cases of all levels of severity went through the courtroom, and various men and women were held in the jail. In one extraordinary case, a trio of burglars earned a good stay at the detention center. The crime took place on March 4, 1919. According to the *Bisbee Daily Review*, a substantial amount of sugar was stolen from Luis G. Sena's store, along with a total of $4,000 worth of merchandise!

A few days after the robbery, Sena was taking a daily stroll on Chihuahua Hill, which is directly behind the city-county building. As he walked along, his eye caught the glare of sunlight hitting and shimmering from a pair of new stockings worn by a young woman who was just in front of him. He was suspicious, since stockings were part of the merchandise that had been stolen from him a few days earlier, so he ran to the office of Marshal Kempton.

Kempton and his assistant, F.E. Thomas, went to investigate. They asked around and found her address. They confronted the woman, Augustine Jaramillo, at her house about her new stockings. Their justification in questioning her was that a bunch of silk stockings were recently stolen from Sena. Where and when did she buy the pair she had on? She denied that they were new and bashfully lifted her skirts to prove so. The officers left abruptly after that display.

But as the men approached the front door to leave, they noticed a bucket of sugar under kindling, nicely stacked near the entrance. Sena told police that at the time of the theft the sugar that had been taken had sage mixed into it. This description matched the condition the sugar was in at the home. Kempton abruptly took Mrs. Jaramillo to jail and left Thomas at the house. Thomas began to look around and discovered that the roof was doubled, meaning it had a fake layer and had a space that was filled with the stolen merchandise!

At that moment, Augustine's husband walked in and was immediately arrested and taken to the jail. He confessed to the robbery and named Manuel Fernandez as his accomplice. Thomas found Fernandez in his home on Naco Road and arrested him as well.

There are countless stories attached to the antiquated building. As a result, it has a great deal of paranormal energy and stirs with an eeriness felt mostly at night. David A. Russel, operations director and business owner of the BTC, said that doors will unexpectedly close and that shuffles around the building can be heard when no one is the vicinity of the strange noises.

At the building's entryway is one of the few original cement staircases left. Under the staircase is another location where a judge used to conduct business. Several guests of the BTC have said that they have seen a lady peering down from the stairwell above the judge's old working space. She has also been seen walking in the hallways.

There is another strange occurrence in the building that many have witnessed and cannot explain. This is the low-toned groans of a man's voice, heard mostly in the dead of night. Many men were sentenced to stay in the cells here, but there was one person who was not an inmate. He was a man who actually worked on the construction of the building in 1918.

According to an article in the *Bisbee Daily Review*, a thirty-six-year-old married man named Frederick Eaton was fatally injured while working

Left: The mysterious apparition of a woman has been seen walking through the hallways of the BTC. *Photo courtesy Bisbee Tourism Center.*

Opposite: Original jail door, an area where eerie groans of a man are heard in the dead of night, possibly those of a man named Eaton. *Photo courtesy Bisbee Tourism Center.*

on the job. A cement stonemason, he was working on the new city-county building when a hook supporting a heavy block used for hoisting stone broke and fell on him. Several of his ribs were broken and splintered. The ends of them penetrated his lungs, causing them to fill with blood.

Eaton died at the Calumet & Arizona Hospital three days after the accident. His death certificate signifies that the injury took place on November 18 and that he died at 5:00 p.m. on the twenty-first. It also gives the cause of death as "injury, right side crushed."

The sounds of a man groaning in the BTC are comparable to those of someone experiencing an accident such as the one Fred Eaton suffered. It may very well be Eaton, still in pain after 102 years, not letting the world forget what was sacrificed for the construction of the building on Naco Road.

COPPER QUEEN HOTEL

The Copper Queen Hotel, completed in 1902, was a swanky place for investors, out-of-town administrators, politicians and rovers to rest their dusty hats while traveling on stagecoaches, trains and, eventually, automobiles. In fact, the hotel was built directly behind the company's general offices as a convenience for the mining officials. It was considered one of the most magnificent acquisitions to Bisbee and lived up to the great industry of the Copper Queen, from which it got its name. This hotel was built by the Copper Queen Mining Company and is the longest continuously operating hotel in Arizona.

The incredible structure has five floors and was built in the old Mission style, entirely appropriate to the Southwest. It took approximately one and a half years to build, and the total expenditure was around $75,000, less than the estimated cost of $100,000. Chas. C. Rouzer, the first manager of the hotel, was from Chicago.

The *Bisbee Daily Review* described the hotel in February 1902. It reported that the flight of stairs as one enters the hotel is made of California redwood and is beautifully paneled. The ladies' bathroom to the right of the front entrance, with a long hall, is made of mahogany, with rich green silk plush and satins. There was a large billiards parlor, a buffet and a barbershop.

To the left of the office was the large dining hall with a seating capacity of seventy-eight persons. In the rear of the room were two private dining rooms for families or private parties for thirty-six guests. Every piece of china and silverware had a special monogram of the hotel. The glassware also had a "C.Q." monogram etched onto them. The first dinner served in the dining room was on February 10, 1902. The building very much mirrored the upscale and ornate style of the RMS *Titanic*. The total bill for the furnishings and decorations was $25,000.

The Arizona & Southeastern depot was going through renovations during the month of January 1902, and the railroad moved its telegraph offices to the hotel until the work was completed.

An odd occurrence took place on the morning of January 19, 1902. A donkey that was worn out from a lifetime of work stretched out right in front of the Copper Queen Hotel and died. Witnesses said his ears drooped and his eyes seemed to go cold, then he collapsed. The coroner said, "Poor John. Your work is done. You have carried your last load of wood. Your sweet thin voice will no longer be heard at a late hour serenading the guests of the Copper Queen. You will be missed."

Copper Queen Hotel. When it was built in 1902, it was considered one of the most modern buildings in town. *Photo courtesy of Jenny Chavez.*

Today, the Copper Queen Hotel has forty-eight rooms available for guests. The dining room is called the 1902: The Spirit Room Fine Dining. The hotel also has its original watering hole, the Overlook Saloon, a private resort pool and many other services for its guests.

Various celebrities have stayed at the Copper Queen over the years, including John Wayne (there is a room named for him), Lee Marvin, the cast of *Young Guns II*, First Lady Nancy Reagan, Jake Lamotta and cast members of *Desperation*, a movie adapted from a Stephen King novel.

The Queen has a few resident ghosts and has become infamous because of the stories attached to it. I was interviewed for SyFy's *Ghost Hunters*, a television show that filmed there in 2006, regarding the paranormal activity at the hotel. I also wrote of my first ghost hunt at the hotel in 2000. Here is an excerpt from *Mi Reina: Don't Be Afraid*.

> *At the Saloon in the hotel my group watched a VCR tape of a recent television interview regarding the hauntings at the hotel. Then the manager at the time told us that the hotel was home to three claimed spirits. A stripper named Julia Lowell who is in her 50s, a man who appears to be in his 80s has been seen and a five-year-old boy who is said to have drowned.*
>
> *The manager said that a guest on the fifth floor had once awakened at 3:15 a.m. to a woman dressed in black. She began to remove her clothing and when the man tried to reach out and touch her, she faded away.*
>
> *"We have had several reports of different experiences by hotel guests. Two years ago, at Thanksgiving time, a table of eight was enjoying a holiday meal in the dining room, when a little girl from the group continued to say she had to stay under a table, because she wanted to play with the little boy. None of the adults could see the entity," said the hotel executive.*

The hotel's manager gave us a more detailed description of the three resident ghosts as he guided us through the building. He said Lowell was actually a prostitute who used the hotel for her wealthy clients. Supposedly, she fell in love with one of her regulars and, after he rejected her, committed suicide. A room is named after her, and some of the reported phenomena related to her ghost is from men claiming to hear a woman's voice whispering in their ear. She touches the feet of men and pulls at their covers while they sleep. She has been most active on the west side of the building and on the second and third floors.

According to a blog post written by the late Michael London, "Who Wrote the Murder of Julia Lowell?," the person named Julia Lowell was written as a character for a Murder Mystery Weekend held at the Copper Queen Hotel in the late 1990s. London was a cowriter and reported that, after the event, the employees and the manager at the time began to fill a ghost ledger daily with anything that sounded believable.

London had a historical walking tour in Old Bisbee and was credited with being accurate in his storytelling. Unfortunately, he passed away a few years ago. In his blog, he stated that he did believe in spirits but to his knowledge no one had died at this hotel and the Queen would only lodge investors or tourists. London wrote that only "respectable" guests would be allowed to stay.

I have researched for any deaths at the Copper Queen Hotel and have not found any reports about a suicide in any decade. If a person had committed suicide at the hotel, it would have made the local newspapers with detailed accounts of the incident.

The second ghost, an elderly man, has been reported to have a beard and is tall and wears black clothing. A reported phenomenon is the smell of a cigar before or after he has been seen. He appears as a full-bodied apparition in doorways and in dark areas of the fourth floor. He has been seen on the elevator or coming off of it one moment, and the next, he simply disappears.

The third ghost is a small boy who is said to have drowned at the San Pedro River, approximately twelve miles from the hotel. Legend says his spirit made its way back to the hotel because his mother was an employee there. He haunts the west side of the building and on the second and third floors.

Reported phenomena of this spirit include objects belonging to guests being moved from one area to the next with no explanation. Pens and keys have levitated in front of people. Guests have heard phantom footsteps of children running up and down the hall with no children around. A loud and gripping giggling sometimes echoes through the halls. Many believe the sound belongs to the ghost child.

OLIVER HOUSE

For over one hundred years, in the historical district of Bisbee, Arizona, a beautifully designed building has stood on a piece of land that looks like an island floating on a high cement retaining wall. This place is called the Oliver House. The establishment was named after the owner, Jane Oliver. Cochise County archives show that, in 1909, she was taxed for an incomplete building, and in 1910, she was taxed for a complete building at the same address. Over the years, the Oliver House was used as a mining office building and, during the Depression, was a men's dormitory. It is now an inn.

Jane Oliver ran the inn by herself until her death in 1912. At that time, her son Richard and his wife, Lilly Belle, took over. Jane Oliver had another son named Thomas, a captain with the Bisbee Fire Department. According to death certificates and newspaper articles archived at the Arizona

Oliver House, a building with an interesting past, with four recorded deaths inside its walls and the infamous shooting of Nat Anderson.

State Capitol, since the Oliver House has been in business, four deaths have occurred there, along with a shooting. The University of Arizona's parapsychology department has performed research labs at the Oliver House and has come up with the same number of deaths.

There has, for several years, been a story of a "mass killing" at the inn. But searches for any evidence of such an event at the establishment have revealed nothing. There is no "Mass Day of Deaths" in the death certificate archive for the Oliver House in Bisbee or at the Arizona State Capitol. Nor is there any documentation of a massacre reported at the inn found at the Bisbee Mining and Historical Museum, at the Cochise County archives or in any newspaper articles.

The recorded deaths at the Oliver House include Jane Oliver, who died on October 10, 1912. A newspaper announcement was published on October 11, 1912, saying that she was the owner and proprietor of the Oliver House and had died at her home.

A baby girl named Constance Hoover, one year of age, died from pneumonia on November 27, 1912, at 4:00 a.m. Her death certificate states that she died at the Oliver House.

George E. Patterson, a thirty-five-year-old salesman, died of illness on December 30, 1913. A *Bisbee Daily Review* article dated December 31, 1913, has the headline "Found Dead on Floor of Room." Patterson was found by Richard Davis, the owner of the Oliver House. Davis had entered Patterson's room the day before at 11:00 a.m. and found him lying on the floor, dead.

Arthur Lewis, a thirty-eight-year-old miner, died of illness on May 22, 1930. His death certificate states that he died at the Oliver House.

Then there is a twenty-eight-year-old roadmaster for the Copper Queen Mining Company who was shot at the Oliver House on February 22, 1920. The shooting was called the "Oliver House Notorious Murder." According to the *Bisbee Daily Review*, Nat Anderson was gunned down by an unknown assailant as he was entering his room in the Oliver lodging house at 3:30 a.m. He died at the Copper Queen Hospital at 1:20 p.m. the same day without ever regaining consciousness. At the time of his death, Anderson had been a roadmaster for two years at the mining company on Sacramento Hill.

A detailed description of the murder was released by police. The first shot probably killed Anderson, as he was struck in the forehead. As he fell, the second bullet hit his chest, causing a severe flesh wound without entering his body. As Anderson lay flat on his face, his killer fired a third bullet into the lower part of his back.

Lilly Belle Oliver reported to police that she heard a man's voice not belonging to Anderson hurl a violent obscenity at the time of the shooting, as though in overwhelming anger. She ran into the hall and saw a stranger run down the stairs but could not give a good description to police.

Kay Ross was a tenant at the lodging house and by trade was a timekeeper at the Sacramento mine. He heard the shooting from his bed. He got up and grabbed his gun and peered into the hall. He saw Anderson lying on the stairway close to the door of his room. No one else was in sight.

Shortly after, policeman Tex Barton appeared on the scene.

Ross told Bisbee police that he had known Anderson for several years and said his friend had a reputation of drinking very little and of having good habits. In addition, Anderson was liked by many. Ross couldn't think of nor knew a motive.

It was known that Anderson had attended a house party just before he was murdered. Police tried to retrace his footsteps between the time he left the party at midnight and the time when he was shot.

A notice ran in the *Bisbee Daily Review* for about three weeks with a $500 reward from the Moose Lodge for the arrest and conviction of Anderson's murderer. This murder is still a mystery as of 2020.

Reports of phenomena at the Oliver House include doors being opened and shut or slammed on their own. Trish Wirth, the owner of the establishment, said she has heard some odd noises and has experienced some temperature waves in different areas of her inn.

Another eerie occurrence is the crying of a baby. During the planning stages for my haunted tour, one of our tour guides mentioned that a couple who was staying the night at the Oliver House said they heard a baby crying most of the evening. They were told that no babies were there. I said I'd check my list of deaths at the Oliver House.

There she was on my list, in black-and-white. One-year-old Constance Hoover died from pneumonia in 1912. Was this confirmation for one of the hauntings at the inn?

Other ghostly accounts include the sound of running water coming from places where there is no plumbing and the sound of firecrackers in the middle of the night. Guests have seen an elderly woman rock in a rocking chair in the "Grandma Room" when no such person was known to be there. Could this be the apparition of Jane Oliver?

A former owner reported that he had heard, in the middle of the night, footsteps walking down the hall and coming through his closed door and entering his room. When he looked, no one was there.

During a paranormal investigation with the MVD Ghostchasers of Mesa several years ago, as we were waiting for a tour of the building, I was sitting on the porch and saw the curtains twice move through one of the front windows. They opened up as if someone were looking out at us. When the housekeeper came out to get us, I asked if there were guests still there. She said, "Nope, everyone is gone and checked out."

As my group was getting a tour of the kitchen area and had just walked through the door into the hall, it suddenly slammed shut. Nobody was in the kitchen. In fact, the employee was the only one there besides our group.

On the second floor, I heard the faint sound of splashing water coming from an empty room. The sound stopped as soon as I walked back into the room.

HOTEL LA MORE

The Bisbee Inn/Hotel La More sits above Brewery Gulch on OK Street and in front of Chihuahua Hill. It is the second-largest hotel in Bisbee and on the site of a large fire that raged through the neighborhood in 1907. The hotel stands on two lots and the site of two houses, later a large wood building. Sometime in 1916, S.P. Bedford built the two-story brick structure on the same location.

In October 1917, the twenty-four-room hotel opened to the public and was leased to Kate La More, who gave the inn its name. She and her husband, Richard, were considered "old timers" from the Warren District. This location was prime in the early days. It was just up the hill from the train depot and steps away from the many saloons and restaurants along Brewery Gulch.

Some of the La More family lived at the hotel, including Maymie La More, Kate's sister, who ran the hotel's annex on the second floor of the Muheim building on Brewery Gulch. In 1925, a woman named Grace Waters purchased and operated it under the Waters name. In the 1960s, the building served as a Peace Corps training facility. It was also used as two-room apartments and housed a Pentecostal group at one time.

In the mid-1980s, Elissa and Al Strati bought the hotel and restored it to its original beauty. They even had the La More sign lettered on the south wall of the building in a style resembling the old ghost signs. They hired Alan Scott of Bisbee to take on that task. The Stratis also bought and tore down a decrepit building next door to the hotel for parking purposes.

The site of the hotel is directly in front of Chihuahua Hill, where, in June of 1907, a gas stove blew up in the kitchen of the Colorado Boarding House at the foot of the same mountain. It was very windy that day, which facilitated the fire. It destroyed seventy-six houses and caused significant damage to thirty more. Only minor injuries were recorded, with no deaths due to the fire. But there was $200,000 worth of damage.

The fire department fought with exceptional valor but had practically no equipment. It had very minimal hoses with low pressure—so low that

Bisbee Inn/Hotel La More. The twenty-four-room hotel was built in 1916 and located on two lots where two residences were destroyed in a fire.

the water couldn't reach the structures. In addition, people in carriages and wagons were driving over the hoses laying on the street.

Finally, the Bisbee miners stepped in. They set up dynamite charges inside houses north of the Pythian Castle, about where Hotel La More stands today. The miners blew up those houses, creating a much-needed firebreak and saving the neighborhood and probably the entire town of Bisbee.

Almost identical to the fortune-teller predicting fires at the Hermitage, another psychic, Emmanule Anderson, predicted this fire, including the exact time, on Chihuahua Hill.

There are many ghost stories attached to this hotel. I described some of them in my book *Mi Reina: Don't Be Afraid*, including a ghost hunt with the MVD Ghostchasers. Here is an excerpt.

The General Manager of the hotel told our group about the paranormal activities recorded there. She said that after so many guests reported strange experiences, we asked them to log them for us. One saw a woman float down one of the stairways, another said she could smell lilac water in her room. Our housekeepers have said that on several occasions after making up a bed and leaving the room, they returned to find it messed up again.

She also informed us the second floor seems to be the most active, especially rooms 14, 15, 16 and 17.

Room 15 has reports of an imprint of a body on the bed in the room and when a person is in that bed, they said they can sometimes feel the weight of someone sitting on the bed.

After the short presentation of alleged hauntings made by the manager, I instinctively made it to Room 15. I stood at the doorway of the empty room, as check out time had just passed, leaving the Inn primarily vacant and a perfect time for the investigators to take a closer look.

As I carefully scanned the room, I called out to the infamous entity.

"Are you here now? Do you want to take a sit with me?" I whispered.

I took a tempting chance and sat at the edge. I waited for an answer from the phantom. I closed my eyes, took in a long and calming breath, hoping to connect with the spirit. In a calm and slow manner, the hair on my body began to rise, as well as my heart rate, as the vibration of footsteps began to approach my location.

"Come, it's all right. I want to talk to you," I quietly said in just above a whisper.—"So, this is the home of the brave spirit huh?" With great disappointment, an older member of the paranormal group interrupted me, as he proceeded to enter the room.

During the investigation, two orbs close to the ceiling were photographed by several members of the group, as if the entities were observing from an elevated position and listening intensely for any information regarding their existence. There were several claimed clairvoyants there with me that day, and we all concurred most of the energy was coming from the hallway of the second floor.

During the time when the Stratis were renovating the hotel, a witness to an eerie experience was invited to coffee and tea, as a soft celebration of the completion of the restoration. She thought the place looked incredible. Sometime during the celebration, she went to use the bathroom. She ventured out into the hotel to find the bathroom on her own and decided to explore a little bit.

She went to a closed door. As soon as she touched the doorknob, she pulled away, because it was extremely hot! It actually burned. She touched the door, and it was very warm. She abruptly went back to her group and said they had better come and check a room she tried to enter, to make sure there was no fire or the beginning of a blaze.

The owner rushed back to the same door and grabbed the handle without any trouble and whipped it open. No fire. She turned around and said that everything was fine. The guest of the tea party touched the door herself and said it was now cool to the touch!

7
LOWELL

L owell is a community one mile southeast of Old Bisbee. It originated in 1901. Upper Lowell was created soon thereafter. It was a fairly densely populated area with a main street. It had its own theater, bakery, saloons, brothels, restaurants and jail that included a justice of the peace.

Although the existence of the Red-Light District had ended in the Upper Brewery Gulch and Zacatecas areas, Lowell had its own. That started around 1904 and lasted until the winter of 1917. The U.S. secretary of war investigated how the women working in Lowell were affecting the soldiers stationed nearby. The secretary directed the city of Bisbee to close Lowell's Red-Light District. The city council complied and voted to close the tenderloin district on December 10, 1917.

Disaster hit on October 11, 1920, when more than half of the town of Lowell was lost to a fire. It was reported that everything on the north side of Main Street and up to Naco Road was destroyed, causing $750,000 in damage. It was believed the fire started somewhere in the back of a meat market and in the smokehouse and spread to the barn and corral of the Brophy Carriage Company. The flames moved from the lower end of Main Street to the yard of the Bisbee Lumber Company.

The *Bisbee Daily Review* reported that the yards at the lumber company formed a vortex, a veritable whirlwind of fire. Flames shot up from the center like a volcano. Explosions from gasoline tanks and cases of ammunition went off with a rattle of rifle fire.

While people tried to salvage their equipment and any merchandise by putting them in the middle of the street, thieves came and took the items and ran. Many of these individuals were arrested on-site. Eventually, the entire business section of Lowell was rebuilt, bigger and more modern than before.

Just as the Sacramento Pit was created and Jigger Ville was dismantled then was blown up, so was Upper Lowell and some of main Lowell itself. When the mining company excavated the area for the Lavender Pit in the 1950s, a large chunk of Lowell disappeared. Only Erie Street is left, and across the way is the Saginaw neighborhood, Evergreen Cemetery and Lowell School.

HEADLESS MINER

The Bisbee mining district had more than fifty mines, including the two open pits, during its existence. The deepest of these goes down to the 3,300-foot level. The Lowell Shaft, in particular, has been a hot topic of conversation since 1905. The headframe and shaft were lost to the Lavender Pit, but it holds one of the most legendary ghost stories in Bisbee.

According to an article in the *Bisbee Evening Miner* in 1909, a miner working at the Lowell Shaft saw a fellow worker lying on top of a pile of timber. The miner went to touch the man to see if he was all right and asked if he was okay. The kind miner began to lift the man from the pile, then a horrifying realization came to the Samaritan. He saw that he had a body in his arms without a head!

Screams of horror echoed through the underground mine tunnels that must've shook dust from the ceilings and walls. The miner dropped the headless body and sprinted in long strides to his home in nearby Bakerville.

The headless ghost was seen at another nearby shaft by two miners. In this case, the two men saw the ghost, looked at each other and continued to work, far away from it.

News spread of the headless ghost sightings. Some believed the story, while others shrugged it off. Even so, the miners were fairly nervous of what was lurking in the darkest corners of the Lowell Shaft and jumped when there was any type of non-work-related noise.

Some of the miners wanted a chance to meet with the headless ghost, but others were happy to forget the idea of running into the horrific spook. The biggest worry was that the ghost would begin to visit all of the shafts in the Warren and Bisbee Districts and cause a panic. The newspaper stated that

The Junction Shaft's headframe at Erie Street. This is what the Lowell Shaft, which sat south of the Lavender Pit, would have looked like.

miners in general are a naturally brave group, but the thought of running into the headless miner was something they could do without.

Reports of the ghost will most likely be shared for decades to come. Unfortunately, hundreds of miners have lost their lives in the Bisbee mines, and there is much assurance that this ghost is not the only one residing in the thousands of miles of tunnel below the town.

LOWELL SCHOOL

There is a large brick building that faces Evergreen Cemetery called Lowell School. It is adjacent to Highway 80, at a very large roundabout. Construction of the school was completed in 1931, and on the first day of school, seven hundred students were enrolled. The school was built for the children from Lowell, South Bisbee, the Johnson Addition and Tin Town.

The front entrance of the school is magnificent, with its set of double doors made of solid copper. They weigh eight hundred pounds and are

The Lowell School, built in 1931. An appealing feature is its two massive copper doors, symbolic of the grandeur of Bisbee's mining industry.

symbolic of the Bisbee mining district. The roof is also made of copper—sixteen tons of it!

There are nineteen large classrooms and lockers on the first and second floors, and the building has a fireproof basement with huge steel doors. At one time, there was a janitor's apartment located on the south side of the first-floor corridor. The apartment had a foyer, kitchenette, dining room, living room, bath and bedroom, with a private entrance.

A large auditorium is located on the west side of the first-floor main corridor. It seats nine hundred and has individual theater chairs on the main floor and balcony. Some time ago, the balcony was closed. The school was constructed by R.E. McKee of El Paso, Texas, and the architectural firm was Lesher and Mahoney from Phoenix. A $200,000 bond was used to pay for the $191,371 construction, including the costs for the property, construction and equipment.

In February 1935, a section of the basement at the school was used by Phillip Sanderson. He was a sculptor commissioned by the Federal Relief Administration to create the *Copper Miner* statue. It is located on Tombstone Canyon Road, in front of the Bisbee Courthouse. He sculpted a two-foot model in Warren, then moved to the school, where most of the work of the statue was completed. Lee Petrovitch was the model for the *Copper Miner* statue. The unveiling of the monument took place on November 11, 1935.

Lowell School is where thousands of Bisbee children have attended elementary and junior high school, including myself. I attended the school from the sixth through the eighth grades.

One classroom in particular, in the area where the janitor's apartment may have been located, has a high degree of paranormal activity. Pasqual Chavez attended Lowell in the 1990s and, during his seventh-grade year, experienced an eerie incident in that classroom.

He said that the teacher instructed her students to open a book to a certain page. Chavez recalled that he didn't want to work and started talking and laughing with other students. Another teacher was standing directly behind him. The first teacher became frustrated, and at that point, Chavez did what he was asked. He found the page in the textbook; as soon as he did, the book slammed shut. On its own! He said he was shocked and the hair on his arms and neck stood up. Chavez even recalled that the hair of a girl sitting in front of him was moved by the draft of the slammed book.

He stood up. The teacher nearest him saw what happened and asked if he did that. He said no.

The people in the room were dismayed and frightened by what they witnessed and talked about it for days. This was witnessed by six students and a teacher.

Chavez also said that the classroom's bathroom light flickered often when a student was inside, and then the light would go off. He said that things like that always seemed to happen in that classroom.

EVERGREEN CEMETERY AND THE VENGEFUL GHOST KEEPING GUARD

Evergreen Cemetery has a special place in the hearts of Bisbee families whose loved ones have been laid to rest there where the hallowed grounds are sacred and cherished with grief and love. This forty-plus-acre cemetery is where the bodies from the old cemetery in Brewery Gulch were transferred. It was officially established on May 3, 1912, with Ordinance 175 of the Bisbee Common Council. It is located in Lowell.

There are many gorgeous tombstones—more like monuments—at the grave sites of Bisbee pioneers. There are also mausoleums for the influential families who settled the community. Of the cemetery's space, 60 percent is allocated to the several fraternal and private organizations that used to thrive in Bisbee. There is a special section for war veterans and a large religious area. There is also a high number of unmarked graves at this cemetery, evidence of the individuals who may have traveled to Bisbee from distant countries with no kin to gift them with a deserved marker—or persons who were alone, in life and in death.

In the older section of Evergreen Cemetery is a family plot that is haunted by a ghost of a man who, for the vengeance of the death of his young daughter, shot and killed a man who he thought was to blame. William C. Greene shot James C. Burnett on Allen Street in Tombstone and was later acquitted of murder charges.

The Greene family was a substantial part of Cochise County history. Ella Roberts Greene's past has been chronicled in two different ways. Some write that she was a widow of William M. Moson from California; others say she divorced the father of her son and daughter in 1880.

At that time, she joined her brother Ed Roberts and his family, then moved to Oregon. Shortly after, they all moved to Arizona with a herd of horses. Ella settled along the San Pedro River and created the OR Ranch, which also housed her large herd of steer. Shortly after, she met her future husband, a miner with the nickname "Colonel" William Cornell Greene, although he was never in the military. They married in Tombstone in 1884.

Ella was irrigating over a hundred acres of bottomland and had dammed the San Pedro River. One sad day, tragedy struck. The couple's ten-year-old daughter, also named Ella, and her friend Katie Cochran were swimming in the San Pedro River below the family dam on June 25, 1897.

Swimming there was something they did often. On this day, the two girls jumped into the water without hesitation. At that moment, a crushing rush of water pushed them down under and both were drowned. Unbeknownst to them, Burnett had blasted the Greene dam with dynamite that day.

For several years before the tragedy, the two men had many controversies and arguments over water lawsuits. There were reports three years before the incident that Burnett threatened to kill Colonel Greene the first chance he got. After the death of his daughter, Greene offered $1,000 for information on who blew up his dam.

At 1:00 p.m. on July 1, 1897, on Allen Street and near the OK Corral stables, Greene's gun expelled three rounds, killing Burnett. Witnesses reported that Burnett's body faced downward in a pool of blood. When his body was turned over, blood spurted from the gunshot wound in his chest.

Colonel Greene was arrested at the site and taken to jail. A reporter from the *Prospector* went to the sheriff's office just a few minutes after the shooting and took a statement from the killer. This is an excerpt of Greene's statement from the newspaper article in the *Graham Guardian* dated July 9, 1897.

> *I have no statement to make other than that man was the cause of my child being drowned. I ascertained beyond the shadow of a doubt that he was the guilty man, and when I thought of my little girl as she put her arms around my neck on the day she drowned, I could think of nothing but vengeance on the man who caused her death. I have lived in this territory twenty-five years and have always been a peaceable, law-abiding man, I held no animosity and have no regret for anything except the death of my little girl, and the little Cochran girl and the grief of my poor wife.*
>
> *He added, "Vengeance is mine, I will repay, saith the Lord."*

Greene had public sympathy in his favor. Friends and bondsmen rushed to pay for his bond, set at $30,000. His trial was short, as several witnesses came forward to testify against Burnett, setting Greene free from murder charges.

There was an agreement of some kind between Greene and the City of Bisbee at the time of his wife's death in December 1899. Greene agreed to fence Evergreen Cemetery if the city promised to keep up his family plot for as long as the cemetery existed.

No known agreement was ever found, but according to a 2003 article in the *Bisbee Observer*, documents were found that seem to match the perpetual care promise. There were reports to the city council from 1917 through 1933 of the Greene plot's condition. These included one dated July 1917 that the fence around Mrs. W.C. Greene's plot was painted and grass cut twice. Another report, from June 1919, stated that the grave of Mrs. W.C. Greene had been cleaned up. In November 1923, the Greene plot was cleaned; in September 1932, it was reported that the Greene plot was looking very lovely. In September 1932, it was said that the Greene plot was looking nice for Memorial Day. During 1965, a first-class job had been done on the Greene plot. There were no more entries on record regarding the upkeep of the family plot after that year.

As mentioned before, Evergreen Cemetery is a much-loved site and is often visited by Bisbee residents at different times of the day. There have been reports of a white fog surrounding the Greene plot on sunshine-filled days. There have also been reports of the sound of hard footsteps, of one person marching on the pavement near the plot.

Greene family plot in Evergreen Cemetery. A tragic drowning turned to resentment and finally murder. "The Lord giveth and the Lord taketh away."

As stated earlier, Lowell School stands across from the cemetery. Over the decades, there have been several accounts of lights being seen at night there. Students arriving from long-distanced away games have said they saw eerie lights floating over graves in the cemetery, in particular in the vicinity of the Greene plot.

Individuals visiting the cemetery have witnessed, usually from a distance from the family plot, an apparition of a man walking around it. When the grave site is approached, the man disappears.

The family plot where the hauntings take place has a tall monument marking the grave for the young Ella. Next to her is her mother's large headstone. There is another grave marker on the ground that reads "Greene" and, a few feet away, a bird sculpture resembling a dove on a square stone block. Greene died in 1911 and is buried in Cananea, Mexico.

Colonel Greene's ghost may be haunting the cemetery plot during the times the city isn't maintaining it and is nowhere to be seen when it is.

8

WARREN

The townsite of Warren, completed around 1907 as part of the City Beautiful movement, was created by the C&A Mining Company. This new area, about three miles southeast of Bisbee, was named after the "Father of Bisbee," George Warren. The company reported that it was imperative that its own employees have a desirable place to build and own homes. At this time, Bisbee was becoming overpopulated, and living conditions had become unacceptable for copper miners and their families.

C&A raised $900,000 through the issuance of stock and started planning for the townsite in May 1905. The concept was for the area to have both functional and aesthetic qualities, including affordable housing, a good water supply, sanitary conditions and education and recreational opportunities.

Warren is not as mountainous as "Old Bisbee" but is still hilly and steep in some areas. It is not as congested as the older area of town, but it very much has gorgeous views and is a pleasant place to visit and to live.

THE CALUMET & ARIZONA MINING COMPANY HOSPITAL BUILDING

The C&A Hospital was a $100,000 model of beauty, comfort and convenience located high on a hill overlooking Warren in the Bakerville neighborhood. The three-story building was considered a modern marvel and a step ahead of any other medical institution in the country. It officially opened on June 9, 1918.

Above: George Warren, also known as the "Father of Bisbee," was the person for whom the Warren District was named.

Opposite: C&A Hospital. This grand building was erected to accommodate a growing population when Bisbee was booming.

The facility was the best money could buy and was built when Bisbee was growing rapidly and needed such a large hospital. The building was placed at a high altitude, at the end of Hillcrest Street, so that mountain breezes during the hotter season could cool down the rooms. The hospital was furnished and designed to make patients and employees comfortable and for all-around quick healing.

The new establishment had forty-two rooms. The operating room, on the third floor, was furnished with the latest appliances and inventions of modern medicine. The nine patient private rooms were decorated in both mahogany and bird's-eye maple, white walls, two big windows and elegant pictures. The windows in all of the rooms had a transom ventilation at the top. The second floor had four wards containing ten beds and one bathroom at each end. There was an X-ray room, reception area, kitchen and dining room. The first floor had a contagious ward. The hospital closed in 1930, when the Phelps Dodge Company merged with the C&A Mining Company.

In later decades, the elaborate hospital was sold and transformed into an apartment building called Hillcrest Apartments. In recent times, the building closed and is currently vacant.

Countless accounts of paranormal activity have been reported over the years. The residents of the apartments have heard doors slamming, screams coming from various floors with no explanations, the sounds of people crying when no one is around and eerie phantom footsteps on every level of the building.

A former resident reported that, every evening at the same time, he heard the sound of feet walking and stopping in front of what seemed like each apartment door. The strides of the footsteps seemed short and quick and belonging to a pair of hard shoes.

One night, he decided to take a look and opened his door just enough to see through the opening. As soon as he peeked, he saw an apparition of a woman in what looked like a nurse's uniform. The ghost was quick and blurred right past him and traveled down the hall, then disappeared.

9

CAMP NACO

THE BARRACKS OF THE BUFFALO SOLDIERS

On July 28, 1866, the U.S. Congress created four all-Black regiments, also known as the Buffalo Soldiers; eventually, six regiments were established. Three of the units—the Ninth and Tenth Cavalries and the Twenty-Fifth Infantry Regiment—were sequestered to Camp Naco, an army post located near Bisbee's city limits. They were sent there to enforce U.S. neutrality laws and to maintain peace and to protect Americans on the border.

The troops responded to border skirmishes as early as 1898, but troops reported to Naco for duty in November 1910, the same year as the Mexican Revolution. According to "Preserving Historic Camp Naco," a preliminary research report compiled by Debby Swartzwelder, the first battle of Naco, Sonora, occurred on May 19, 1911. Even though it occurred in Mexico, this event showed the United States that conflict along the border was inevitable. Vigilance would be necessary to protect U.S. interests.

The military post began as a large tent camp. The construction of the permanent adobe compound consisting of twenty-three buildings began in 1915, 1916 or 1917. The camp was at least thirty to forty acres, based on references in quartermaster documents, but the lease of the property identifies the size as approximately ten acres.

The post has been called different things, but Camp Naco is the likely name of the compound during the military's use of the area. Some do refer to this site as Camp Newell or Newell's Camp, to honor John J. Newell, one of the original landowners of the Naco townsite and owner of the land the camp is on. The property was leased to the U.S. government for one dollar with the understanding that the land would be returned to the Newell family when the government no longer needed it.

Five thousand troops had served at Camp Naco. A Los Angeles newspaper reporter wrote in 1914 that forty-five men and women had been shot and killed by stray bullets along the border and near Camp Naco. In 1914, the Associated Press reported that Private Leroy Bradford, Troop B, Tenth Cavalry, was killed in Naco, Arizona, in a battle with Yaqui Indians.

In June 1919, the U.S. War Department planned a $7 million border fence, with the soldiers providing the show of force for the fence. The camp closed in 1923.

The camp was used by the Civilian Conservation Corps in the mid-1930s, and the property also housed workers during the Depression. In 1990, VisionQuest, an organization that uses alternative treatments for juveniles in trouble, took ownership of the property with intentions to preserve the history of the Buffalo Soldiers and African Americans.

Huachuca City, Arizona, a community located near Fort Huachuca, purchased the camp for one dollar from VisionQuest in 2006. Huachuca City, Friends of Camp Naco and the Naco Heritage Alliance Inc. are striving to preserve the site's historic integrity while adapting the buildings of Camp Naco for future use.

On May 21, 2006, a fire destroyed four of the smaller buildings of Camp Naco. In the past, the compound has been the victim of vandalism. To deter more damage and to protect the public from harm, the old army post is now surrounded by a chain-link fence.

A paranormal investigation seemed to be the natural thing to do at Camp Naco. Our group, composed of five investigators, was let through the locked gates to the camp by the late Huachuca City mayor, George Nerhan. We wandered the areas of the camp that were not indicated as off-limits by Nerhan.

Kenton Moore, a member of MVD GhostChasers who is also a carpenter and has worked in construction for most of his life, could not stop admiring the detailed craftsmanship of the buildings.

We focused on the old hospital to begin our investigation. Several photographs were taken as each person went through the empty rooms. We went to the rear of the building to begin our first electronic voice phenomena (EVP) work of the night.

Most of the questions—directed to any entity still bound to the building— were asked with the military in mind. I was recorded asking if any of the

Interior shot of a barrack at Camp Naco, where Buffalo Soldiers slept, talked and wrote home over one hundred years ago.

spirits were at the camp because of battles. A faint "yes" could be heard. But when I asked if the entity was injured, an abrupt echoing "no" was heard from another area of the building. A few seconds after that, a clear but soft "no" was also recorded. At the same site of the EVP, a bright and luminous orb was photographed by Moore.

We made our way to where the soldier barracks are located and to the left of the hospital. Here, we did more EVP work and used a pendulum as an instrument to communicate with any spirits lurking in the area. The spirit is directed to answer "yes" or "no" by different swinging motions. It can be forward for "yes" or side to side for "no."

I read a list of questions designed for a Buffalo Soldier who had served at the camp to spark any memories he may have. While Debe Branning, director of MVD GhostChasers, held the pendulum, I read information I had obtained from *Huachuca Illustrated* (volume 1, 1993).

I mentioned the names of Captain Herman Sievert, who commanded Troop A of the Ninth Cavalry in 1913, and Colonel William Brown. He led four troops of the Tenth Cavalry and arrived at Camp Naco in October 1914.

I also read how crowds of visitors from Bisbee and Douglas came near the camp by carts, wagons and horseback to witness the battles. I mentioned that the soldiers arrived in Naco by the Southern Railroad. During one of the battles there, several gunshots had hit buildings, and four troopers were wounded and a horse and one mule were killed.

I asked if any spirit there knew that the Indians gave the soldiers the name Buffalo Soldiers and that the Germans called them "Hell Fighters." The pendulum began to swing "yes" to that question.

Branning asked the spirit if his bed was in the area where we were standing. He directed us to a space a few feet from where we were. We began to recite the alphabet and asked the spirit to tell us the first letter of his name. The pendulum finally swung "yes" to the letter *H*. Different names beginning with the letter *H* were mentioned, and the spirit said "yes" to the name Harry. We couldn't get an answer for his last name.

The questions continued, with Randy Powers asking "Harry" what troop had been barracked there. "Was it Alpha Troop?"

"Yes," was the answer.

"Was Charlie Troop next door?"

Branning said the spirit was getting excited due to the hard swinging of the pendulum to the answer "no."

Randy Powers asked Harry if his job was the troop guide on bearer, which is who carries the troop's pennant. The pendulum swung no.

A haunting Camp Naco before renovations. The site is endowed with an extraordinary story and is cherished by historians.

After that, the pendulum began to slow down to any more questions—a sign that the spirit might be growing tired. Even though the spirit did not answer the last two questions, he did display an intelligent response to what his job may have been. A white glowing orb was photographed in the same building where Harry had communicated with us.

We left those barracks and continued on to another set of living quarters located directly across from that building. Other photographs showing orbs were taken, but no other exceptional evidence was made.

This old military installation is a reminder of the great men who policed the border with honor and integrity. The Buffalo Soldiers are a large part of the U.S. Army's history and of Cochise County history. The continued restoration of Camp Naco and the future endeavors of its caretakers will highlight the men who lived there by showcasing their everyday lives. This will also preserve the history of the persons who served the country and preserve their individual light for future generations.

BIBLIOGRAPHY

Arizona Daily Star. "Bisbee Woman Dies in Shooting Mishap." October 14, 1935.

———. "Former Cochise Jurist Is Dead." July 1, 1945, 9.

Arizona Genealogy Birth and Death Certificates. Arizona Department of Health Services. "Arthur Lewis." May 22, 1930.

———. "Constance Hoover." November 27, 1912.

———. "Federick Eaton." November 18, 1918.

———. "George Marz." July 1, 1909.

———. "James C. Burnett." July 1, 1897.

———. "Jane Oliver." October 10, 1912.

———. "Louis Maure." December 25, 1904.

———. "Mabel Watters." October 13, 1935.

———. "Nat Anderson." Febuary 22, 1920.

Arizona Legislature. "Senate Resolution No. 7." *Journal of the Senate* 6 (1923): 157 and 158.

Ascarza, William. "Mine Tales: Discoverer Failed to See Potential Value of Copper Queen Deposit." *Arizona Daily Star*, February 12, 2017.

———. "Trolleys Popular with Early Southern Arizona Miners." *Arizona Daily Star*, October 11, 2015.

Austin, Noah. "School House Inn." *Arizona Highways* (2015).

Baillie, Amanda. "Ghosts of Bisbee Past." *Vitality Magazine* (December 2015).

Bell, Bob Boze. "Blazing Bastards, Five Clifton Cowboys vs the Town of Bisbee." *True West* (August 2013): 40–43.

Bisbee Daily Review. "All Women and Children Keep Off Streets Today." July 12, 1917.

———. "And Not a Thing Done About It—The Stench Hole Maintained in This City by the County of Bisbee." May 18, 1904.

———. "Bisbee Has Three-Quarters Million Fire Loss." October 15, 1908.

———. "Body of Mexican Is Found Yesterday in McDonald Reservoir." August 19, 1921.

———. "Branch Jail Accepted Fund for Inspection." January 21, 1905.

———. "Branch Jail in a Terrible Way." May 5, 1904.

———. "Brave Fireman Is Dead." July 2, 1909.

———. "Brief City News—Jail Construction Delayed." August 6, 1904, 5.

———. "Brief Local Items." October 11, 1912.

———. "Brisk Warren Building Boom." September 6, 1919.

———. "Brought Head from Battle." April 26, 1913.

———. "Burro Police Rounds Up Animals for City." January 18, 1919.

———. "Children's Playground Looks Practically Assured Thing." December 8, 1912.

———. "City Prepares for Removal of Bodies to Evergreen Plot." January 10, 1915.

———. "County Encroaching on Private Property." July 21, 1904.

———. "County Supervisor Solid for a New Jail." May 20, 1904.

———. "Dilapidated Graveyard or Children's Playground, Which?" February 2, 1913.

———. "Discoverer Geroge Warren First Locator in District." August 6, 1905.

———. "Down Comes the Filthy Old Vermin Infested Jail." May 20, 1904.

———. "The Fair Store Is Noteworthy." December 21, 1913.

———. "Fair Store Opens New Home Tomorrow." October 3, 1909.

———. "Fatal Cough Ends All." October 3, 1905, 1.

———. "Fire Imperils Hot Tamale Industry." March 4, 1911.

———. "Found Dead on Floor of Room." December 31, 1913.

———. "Fred Eaton Dies." November 22, 1918.

———. "Funeral of Mrs. Oliver." October 13, 1912.

———. "Funeral of Nat Anderson." Feburary 22, 1920.

———. "Ghostly Visitations Are Disturbing Zacatecas." October 17, 1909, 8.

———. "Haunted House; Mexicans Say Spooks Visit Former Home of Murdered Man in Bisbee." April 11, 1906: 5.

———. "Hermitage's Opening Will Be Swell Place." May 3, 1904.

———. "Hospital Opening." June 8, 1918.

———. "Hutchinson, Smart Buy Pythian Castle, Old Jail." February 2, 1973.

———. "In Council Chambers." December 19, 1918.

———. "Is Ghost Killer." May 1, 1906.

———. "John Wayne Museum Is Set Here." April 25, 1974.

———. "John W. Ross Has Been Made Justice and Has Accepted." November 12, 1918.

———. "Joseph Muheim, Sr., Pioneer Bisbeean Who Helped Found Cananea, Succumbs at Douglas." March 18, 1951.

———. "Leading Pursuits—Copper Queen Hotel Now Open." Feburary 9, 1902.

———. "Leading Pursuits—The Fair-Frankenberg Brothers and Newman." February 22, 1902.

———. "Local Section." May 10, 1914.

———. "Maybe They Didn't Do Things." May 10, 1904.

———. "Meeting Decides to Get Busy at Once on Petition." September 21, 1918.

———. "Mexican Youth Drowns While Bathing in Reservoir; Efforts to Recover Body Unsuccessful." August 18, 1921.

———. "A Monument to Bisbee's Progress." July 28, 1904.

———. "Monument to Mark Newly Found Grave of George Warren." March 22, 1914.

———. "Mrs. Jane Oliver Dies." October 11, 1912.

———. "Murder of Anderson Baffles Police." Feburary 24, 1920.

———. "Negroes Will Perhaps Have Own School." March 2, 1910.

———. "New C&A Hospital Formally Opens Today." June 9, 1918.

———. "New Calumet & Arizona Hospital Is Model of Beauty, Comfort, Sanitation and Convenience." June 23, 1918.

———. "New Hotel Opens." September 2, 1917.

———. "New Jail a Fine Structure." July 24, 1904.

———. "New School to Oust Cemetery of Early Days." July 11, 1912.

———. "Notice to Architects." June 2, 1904.

———. "Notice to Architects." July 7, 1904.

———. "Notice—$500 Offered by the Moose Lodge." March 3, 1920.

———. "Outside Aid Offered but Not Needed." October 16, 1908.

———. "Owner of the Grand Here and Jacks Will Rebuild." October 20, 1908.

———. "Park Dedication to Take Place May 21; Big Time Is Planned." May 9, 1916.

———. "Park Question Now Squarely Up to the People of City." December 13, 1914.

———. "Playground Plans Meet Delay till Attorney Reports." January 19, 1913.

———. "Playground to Be Supported." October 3, 1912.

———. "Political Section." October 5, 1911.

———. "Raging Flames Sweep Town of Lowell; Loss $750,000." October 12, 1920.

———. "Raid House That Is Near School." April 23, 1912.

———. "Rail Road Man Is Shot Down." Feburary 22, 1920.

———. "Record Goes Smash with Conviction of Douglas Bootlegger." August 17, 1916.

———. "Regular Guard at Jail." January 28, 1905.

———. "Removal of Bodies to Evergreen Is Nearly Complete." January 21, 1915.

———. "Review Man Locked Up." May 18, 1904.

———. "Shortsighted, Selfish, Premature Is Mayor's Stand, Says Merchant." March 2, 1915.

———. "Silk Stockings on Woman Land 3 in Jail as Burglars." March 5, 1919.

———. "Social Hygiene Worker Fails to Find Much Vice in Bisbee Lists Places of Prostitution." March 25, 1921, 1.

———. "Spectacular Sunday Fire." November 11, 1913.

———. "Steel on the Way." August 14, 1904.

———. "Supervisors Refuse to Appoint Additional Justice of the Peace at Douglas." January 12, 1905, 1.

———. "Swallowed Carbolic Acid Woman Takes Deadly Drug by Mistake." September 22, 1905.

———. "1200 I.W.W. Deported from District by Citizens." July 13, 1917.

———. "Widow, Grieving Over Death of Husband, Believed to Have Suffered Loss of Her Mind." May 27, 1921.

———. "Woman Tries to Shoot Paramour Gets 90 Days." August 6, 1912.

———. "Yesterday a Burro Died." January 30, 1902.

Bisbee Evening Miner. "Headless Spook in the Mines." December 11, 1909.

Bisbee Historical Press Booklet. Bisbee, AZ: Bisbee Historical Tours, 2015.

Bisbee School District No. 2. *Lowell School Dedication Booklet*, 1931.

Borderland Chronicles. "Tribute to Those Hard-Rock Miners' Is in Need of Repairs." June 3, 1984.

———. "Woman Afraid to Dance on Dead as Bisbee City Park Dedicated." May 11, 1986.

Border Vidette. "Is Out of Bonds." July 10, 1897.

———. "Tombstone Tragedy." July 3, 1897.

Branning, Debe. "The Ghost Returns Nightly." *Examiner* (2014).

Burgess, Opie Rundle. *Bisbee Not So Long Ago*. San Antonio, TX: Naylor Company, 1967, 1976.

City of Bisbee. *City of Bisbee Comprehensive Transportation Plan—Final Report*. Task Assignment MPD 34-10. Bisbee, Arizona, 2012.

Cochise County Courthouse—Dedicated 1931, Renovated 2000. Commemorative Booklet. Tucson, AZ: Merry Carnell Schlecht, n.d.

"Copper Mining and Landscape Evolution: A Century of Change in the Warren Mining District, Arizona." *Journal of AZ History* (1982): 267–98.

Corbett, Mary Ellen. "Aldofo D. Vasquez Dies June 14 After Lengthy Illness." *Bisbee News*, June 22, 2000.

———. "Adolfo Vasquez' 'Miracle Hill' Overlooks Town's Many and Varied Religious Shrines." *Bisbee News*, November 9, 1995.

———. "Miner's Love Story: 1906." *Bisbee News* 1999.

Cox, Annie M. *History of Bisbee: 1877 to 1937*. Master's thesis. University of Arizona, Tucson, 1938.

Duncan, James F. "Stories of the Early Days of Cochise County." *Bisbee Daily Review*, November 26, 1911, 1, 4.

Evergreen Cemetery Information, Regulations, Map and Cemetery History of Bisbee, Arizona Memorial Site. n.d.

"Ft. Newell." Blue Horse Production and Vision Quest National, n.d.

Graham Guardian. "The Greene Burnett Murder." July 9, 1897.

Kalambakal. "Prostitutes." *The Busy Belles of Bisbee*. n.d.

Kansas City Star. "Score Bisbee Deportation." November 25, 1917.

London, Michael. London's Walking Tour. February 4, 2013. www.londonswalkingtour.blogspot.com.

Maklary, Fran. *Mi Reina: Don't Be Afraid*. Baltimore, MD: Publish America, 2004.

The Oasis. "Outside Opinion." July 24, 1897.

———. "A Tragedy at Tombstone." July 3, 1897.

PARA—Bisbee Final Report. Bisbee, Arizona, 2012.

Patience, Wes. *Bune to Bisbee and Back: A Swedish Family's Pilgrimage 1883–2004*. Phoenix, AZ: Cowboy Miner Productions, 2005.

Powers, Fran. "Bisbee Fire Station No. 2." *Spirits of Cochise County* (August 2009).

———. "Buffalo Soldiers at Camp Naco." *Spirits of Cochise County* (June 2009).

———. "Haunted History—Bisbee Fire Station No. 2." *Bisbee Observer*, October 16, 2013.

———. "Haunted History—Bisbee Oliver House." *Bisbee Observer*, February 18, 2015.

The Prospector. "Admitted to Bail." July 8, 1897.

———. "Funeral of James C. Burnett." July 2, 1897.

———. "On Habeas Corpus." July 7, 1897.

Pyle, Kevin, Cochise County Treasurer Office. "Historic Property Inventory Form for Cemeteries and Graves." N.d.

Ring, Bob, and Al Ring. *Warren Arizona—The City Beautiful.* Pinetop: Arizona History Convention, 2001.

Selig, Elaine Booth. "Maryland Couple Preserving Details of Hotel LaMore's Historical Past." *Bisbee News*, May 21, 1998.

Sobin, Harris. "St. Patrick's Catholic Church Bisbee, Arizona—A History." *St. Patrick's Catholic Church Bisbee, Arizona.* Tucson, AZ: AIA, 1998.

———. Edited by Kathryn Leonard and William S. Collins, based on draft by Harris. National Register of Historic Places Registration Form. Bisbee Residential Historic District. Phoenix, August 25, 2010.

Swartzwelder, Debby. "Preserving Historic Camp Naco." n.d.

Thorp, Cora. "Some of the Teachers in Bisbee from 1881 to 1908." *Cochise County Quarterly* (1974): 9–10.

Tombstone Epitaph. "Bisbee Column." February 23, 1892.

———. "Find No Clues to Killing Nat Anderson." Feburary 29, 1920.

———. "I.W.W.'S Ordered Taken to Columbus, NM." July 15, 1917.

———. "A Tragedy." July 2, 1897.

———. "Will Maintain Office." February 9, 1919.

Tucson Citizen. "Shifting Fortunes Steered Character to Ironic Honor." April 18, 1988.

Tucson Daily Citizen. "In the Ashes of Bisbee Fire, Freedom of the Press Glows." July 30, 1976.

University of Arizona Web Exhibit. "The Deportation of 1917." 2005, University of Arizona.

Vaughan, Tom. "Devastating Fires of 1907 & 1908." *Borderland Chronicles*, July 17, 1983.

———. "First County Jails in Bisbee Not Fit for Men or Animals." *Borderland Chronicles*, May 17, 1987.

———. "The Last Chapters: Major-Fires Saga." *Borderland Chronicles*, July 24, 1983.

Webb, Catharine. "The 'Greene Plot' and Other History." *Bisbee Observer*, November 27, 2003.

Wolhart, Ron. "Through the Fair Window." 2015. Bisbee Restoration Museum.

Ziegler, Jack. "St. Patrick Church, A History." *SEAZ Chronicles Magazine* (n.d.).

ABOUT THE AUTHOR

Photo courtesy of Zoya Greene.

Francine Powers is an Arizona Newspaper Foundation award-winning reporter. She was owner-operator of Bisbee Historical Haunted Tours from 2013 to 2016 and a member of the MVD Ghostchasers from Mesa, Arizona. Powers has been on *Ghost Hunters*, *Streets of Fear* on Fearnet.com, AzFamily 3TV from Phoenix and Tucson's *Morning Blend*. She has been featured in numerous newspaper articles and on radio and podcast shows discussing Bisbee's history and its paranormal activity. She was also highlighted in the magazine *Vitality*, published by the *Sierra Vista/ Bisbee Daily Review*, for her ghost tour. Francine was the editor in chief of her own online paranormal magazine, *Spirits of Cochise County*. The publication covered the history and reports of paranormal activity in southeastern Arizona. She is a Bisbee native and author of *Mi Reina: Don't Be Afraid* (2004), the first ghost book of its kind in Bisbee.

Visit us at
www.historypress.com